Journeys of Healing with the Puzzle Master

ANN GROSS

Outskirts Press, Inc.
Denver, Colorado

Outskirts Press
http://www.outskirtspress.com

ISBN-10: 1-4327-0500-8
ISBN-13: 978-1-4327-0500-8

Library of Congress Control Number: 2007924109

Printed in the United States of America

To Shawna, My Soul-Friend

It is because of YOU and those infamous words "write me a story" that this book and I even exist.
Thank YOU for teaching me to FLY!

Thank you for all the Healing
you have provided to the infants.
This Healing talent is the greatest
legacy you can bring to the new NICU.

Annie

Contents

Part 1

Destiny's Path

Chapter 1

First Steps

The meeting of our Spirits was not a random act. The Universe had been guiding us together for most of our lifetime. For only the Universe could have coordinated precisely the "chance" encounters which led us to each other. Deepak Chopra and other quantum physicists would call it "Universal Synchronicity." Yet as great as the divine Universal Plan was, we both had free will to reject or accept each leg of our journey. How grateful and thankful I am that we both chose to follow that divine map.

My journey to the Puzzle Master began some 50 years ago when my parents had the foresight to move from Maryland to Colorado and in so doing became the "black sheep" of the family. In the late '50s one just did not move far from their immediate family. According to the "family" we might as well have moved to China or Tibet; the distance was the same to them.

Yet now we had the freedom to "Be." No longer did we have to conform to the expectations of others. My parents opened the gate to the proverbial box we had been living in and said "Welcome to your new playground." I was free to think, to do, to be what ever I wanted, or so I thought.

Chapter 2

Rest Stop

From as far back as I could remember I had wanted to be a nurse. Well that is not totally accurate; I knew I wanted to help people or animals. I did not know that the Universe and others of this like mind would give the name "Healer" to this desire. What ever its name, I knew that it was at the core of my being.

At first I wanted to be a veterinarian but my mother told me that since I was a "girl" and we didn't have the money to send me to college; my dream would have to change. At that particular moment in time; at the age of twelve; my Heart was broken by those words.

Another choice would have to be made. What was it that I could do to fulfill this desire, this need to help others? I chose the best career I could think of; I decided to become a nurse. I asked "Would that be ok?" "Yes," I was told.

"That you could do."

From junior high on I planned my classes around going to nursing school. I took every biology and science class I could find. For Christmas I would ask for things like *The Invisible Man*; a clear plastic replica of the human body with organs that I spent hours painting to match the real organs. I asked for a chemistry set and a biology set. I spent countless hours of bliss looking at every thing from dirt to skin under the microscope. I was obsessed with what was "inside."

I wanted to know how everything worked. My mom couldn't understand how I could spend hours dissecting the frog that came in my biology set. The smell of formaldehyde which preserved the frog in it's tiny jar not Pine-sol permeated our kitchen for over a year. She was not too pleased when I ruined her best kitchen knife because I wanted to see what was inside Goldie the goldfish; after it died of course. She finally put her foot down when I came home with a dead cat in my red Radio Flyer wagon.

"What have you got? Did you touch that thing?" she asked in that tone of voice only a mother can produce.

"It's a dead cat I think," I answered. "It got hit by a car up on Garrison. I didn't want to leave it there so other cars could run over it. So since it is dead already, could I have a knife so I can see the rest of what is inside?"

"YOU MAY NOT!" a disgruntled voice yelled. "You are not going to use my good knives on some dead cat. And no you can not carve it up. And don't ever bring another one home. Do you hear me? Now what are you going to do with it?"

"I guess bury it in the back yard," I said disappointedly. I spent the next two hours digging a grave for the unfortunate cat. I said a prayer for him as I placed him in his grave. Some how I knew that he would come back as a kitty once again. I told him to learn from this experience. "Next time you will know that running in front of cars is not good. Or maybe you just need to learn to run faster. Say Hi to God for me when you see Him." And with that I covered him up with the dirt I had so painstakingly dug from Mother Earth. Needles to say, that was the end of my dissection career.

I never settled on my dream of becoming a nurse. As "fate" would have it I met a girl named Diane in Girl Scouts. She wanted to be a nurse as well. On camping trips snuggled inside our sleeping bags we would discuss what it would be like and where we would go. She had already applied to a nursing school in St. Louis, Missouri. "Why don't you come there too," she said excitedly. "We could be room mates and everything. Can you imagine the fun we could have?"

That very next day I wrote the school for an application. It was the only school I requested an application from. Within weeks I received an answer "You have been accepted into the Class of 1971." I was more than ecstatic. I think I jumped five feet in the air as I pumped my fist in celebration and shrieked "Yes! I'm going to nursing school."

My mother waited until I landed firmly back on the ground before saying, "And how are you going to pay for this school? Do you have any money?"

"No" I said. "I thought you and dad would pay for it."

"I told you before, we don't have the money to send you to college. You will just have to write to them and tell them you can't come now. And I suggest you go find a job if you really want to go to nursing school."

I was devastated. I was angry. Actually I was down

right pissed. I thought my dream had been destroyed once again. I thought to myself "Why didn't you tell me this before? Why did you wait until I was accepted into school before you told me about the money?"

Then the humiliation began. I had to call Diane and tell her "I couldn't come that year." Diane understood. "Maybe this will work better," she said. "This way I can be your "Big Sister" and help you since I will be a year ahead of you. It might be even more fun. Don't worry about it, okay?"

I had to write to the school and tell them "Due to financial difficulties I would not be able to attend this year. Would it be possible to change my start date to the next year?" And now I had to find a job.

The school was more than understanding. They wrote back a letter which said "We will place you in the Class of 1972. We look forward to seeing you in September." That was a relief. At least I was still enrolled in a school. My dream was a year farther away but still attainable.

There was still the challenge of finding a job. How could I make enough money in less than a year to go to school. I read through it seemed hundred of ads in the paper. It seemed I wasn't qualified to do anything, I was just out of high school. I applied to be a waitress; "No experience. Sorry," was the usual response. I tried to sell time shares over the phone. That was a disaster. It was the only job I was ever fired from. Communication was not my strong suit back then; especially not the verbal variety. By the end of September I was beginning to panic; I still hadn't found a job. Time seemed to be running out.

We had a routine in our house on Sundays. It was the day Dad would make us pancakes. Sometimes he would make our initials. Sometimes he would put bacon in the middle and pour the batter around it making a "bacon sandwich." Sometimes he would just make funny shapes. I was twelve before I realized that most people's pancakes were just round. I felt sorry for them. They had no idea what they were missing.

After breakfast we would read the Sunday paper. Us kids would take the comics of course. It was a rule that they could not be read unless they were spread out across the entire living room floor. Mom took the ads and clipped coupons with the special "paper only" scissors. And Dad; he would always actually "read" the paper. He handed me the help wanted ads and said "Look again. You might just find something this time."

As I read through the ads, one seemed to just jump out at me, as if it was bolder print than the others, although it wasn't. "Help wanted," it said. "No experience necessary. Will Train. Opportunity for advancement. Apply at Jolly Rancher Candy Factory."

I was there Monday morning at 9:00 am. I handed them my application and they said "When would you like to start? We have an opening on the evening shift. You will get a differential." I cocked my head like a small puppy as I looked at the manager questionably as I had little knowledge of work force language. "It means you get more money."

"I'll take it," I said with gusto. I was now part of the work force, earning money towards my dream.

I accomplished that dream in June of 1975. I graduated from nursing school as a Registered Nurse. There was now a second part to the dream and that was to work with children, babies actually. I wanted to work not in just any hospital. I wanted to work in the prestigious Children's Hospital in Denver.

Chapter 3

Human Angels

After graduation I accepted a job in the hospital where I trained. I would be working in the newborn nursery. It would not be at the hospital of my dreams but I would be working with the babies. My original plan was to stay for one year. I thought I would have a better chance to reach my goal of working at Children's Hospital if I had some experience. One year turned into two and before I knew it three years had passed.

The synchronicity of the Universe is a beautiful thing. It seems to me; now looking in retrospect; that when we stray from our path or we run too far ahead or behind of the divine schedule, the Universe sends in human angels to get us back on track. They guide us with a Universal compass and a Universal watch which has no correlation to man made Time; for that time is run by watches and calendars.

These angels often times go as quickly as they arrived. At other times they stay until we are securely back on the path. It took several of these angles to led me back to the Puzzle Master.

Nurses made a decent salary in those days but it was challenging to live alone. My best friend Kathy and I decided to share an apartment. It made life much more comfortable sharing rent and splitting food costs. We had a far better apartment in a far better neighborhood than either of us could afford alone.

We did most everything together. We worked the same shift; nights; and so we were able to car pool and share the cost of gas.

The arrangement work well for two years. Then it all began to unravel.

Kathy met the love of her life, Michael. He was a genuinely nice guy. It didn't take long before they were deeply involved. They quickly were in the state of bliss where they couldn't keep their hands off each other. This meant that every night we had off there was an overnight guest. As soon as dinner was over, as they were still swallowing their last bite of food they would grab each others hand and head for the bedroom upstairs. It made for a very uncomfortable situation for me.

At first, I tried to occupy myself with doing the dishes but it did not drown out the sounds. Next I tried turning up the volume of the television in order not to hear the squeaking of bed springs and the moans coming from overhead. It was only a temporary fix as the neighbors began to complain of the noise.

I was not one who liked to do things by myself, but it seemed I had no choice. I began going to the mall as soon as dinner was complete. I was such a regular visitor to the electronics shop that they would turn the televisions to my favorite program.

Often times I would pop into the movie theater. The movie that was playing was of no consequence. It was a place where I could think, meditate. One night I closed my eyes and said to God "I can't take this anymore. Tell me what to do?"

Moments later; in a voice neither male nor female I heard "Change your days off." Simple, direct and to the point. As I considered this "suggestion" it made great sense. With this plan I would have two nights off when Kathy would be at work; two glorious, quiet, peaceful nights. Why hadn't I thought of that myself? It was a simple solution.

The next day I presented my plan. I approached it as this would be better for them. It would give them more privacy. I told her that since it was my idea that I would change my schedule. She hardly glanced my way before saying, "Sounds good. Oh, by the way, Michael is moving in this weekend. We need to switch rooms since you have the bigger room. The two of us just can't stay in my room. So we'll switch on Saturday, okay?" And with that she walked out of the house.

It was better having different nights off. It gave me a chance to get to know Michael; at least more than just small talk at the dinner table. Now when Kathy was at work, Michael and I would pop popcorn and watch movies; at home; with a reasonable sound level. We would have conversations about philosophy, what was happening in the world. I was beginning to actually enjoy my nights off.

After a few months Kathy began to change. She was becoming paranoid and jealous. One night she actually accused me of sleeping with Michael. I was shocked. I thought we were better friends than that. I thought she knew me better.

I told her "Michael is your boyfriend. As far as I am concerned he is off limits to me. I would never do that to you, don't you know that? How could you even think that? We just watch TV and talk. That's ALL!" To this day I don't think she believes me.

It was the final push I needed. I knew I had to move out, back to Denver. I couldn't stay here any longer.

Just in case I had any doubts about moving back to Colorado; the Universe made me an offer I couldn't refuse. It came in the form a phone call three nights later.

Chapter 4

Back on Track

That night at work I received a phone call. To my surprise it was my Dad. Phone calls in the middle of the night from one's parent is usually never a good sign I thought to my self. So I asked him "What's wrong Dad?"

"Your mother is sick. I need you to come home. She is asking for you. I booked you a flight in the morning. It leaves at 9:00am."

"Dad, tell me what's wrong. Why is she sick? Where is she?"

"Well," he paused not wanting to worry me, "She's in the hospital. Shae had a heart attack and is in intensive care. She keeps asking for you. We need you here," he finished with a quite desperation in his voice.

"Okay" I said trying to hold back the tears. "Tell her I'll be there in the morning. I love you Dad."

"I love you too," he choked out. "I'll pick you up at the airport and then we'll go straight to the hospital."

"See you in the morning," I said as I hung up the phone. I could no longer contain my tears. My back followed the contour of the desk as I slid to the floor, tears streaming down my face. Kathy found me there, in a pile on the floor. I told her what had happened, how I needed to get "home." She called the nursing supervisor who willingly took over for me.

I raced home and in less than 30 minutes packed a suitcase with whatever clothes I could find; a few shirts, jeans, underwear and drove directly to the airport. I sat in hard plastic chairs, immune to their discomfort; or paced the corridor for four anxious hours waiting for my plane. Time seemed to be standing still.

I stayed with mom for a week until she was out of intensive care. She was very weak; even walking a few steps made her short of breath. Mom needed someone to stay with her once she got home. Dad had to work and my little sister; then 13, needed someone to look after her as well. My other two sisters were at college. I couldn't ask them to give up their dreams when I had already completed mine. That non gendered voice inside my head said "It's time to come home."

I reassured mom that I would be back. "I need to give two weeks notice at work then I will be back for good. I promise." Two weeks later to the day, my dad and I were on the road driving a U-haul trailer filled with all my worldly possessions back to Denver.

The most curious thing is that Kathy and I never remained in contact after I moved. It was as if we dropped out of each others lives. I think it was because she had finished her angel work. She had gotten me back to Denver where I needed to be; one step closer to the Puzzle Master.

Chapter 5

An Angel Returns

I returned home in April of 1978. Mom was still recovering from her hear attack. It took hours for her to just get up and get dressed. Taking care of the house, cooking and cleaning were out of the question for her. These were now my responsibilities.

During the quite times between vacuuming and laundry I remembered that my friend Diane had moved back to Colorado after graduation. We had lost contact with each other during those three years I was in St. Louis. I tried looking her up in the phone book but found no number. Several days later, while cleaning out a closet, I just "happened" to find a list of phone numbers from my old girl scout troop. Diane's old home number was on the list.

I took the chance that her parents hadn't moved and dialed the number. Her mother answered and remembered me. "Yes; you were in Girl Scouts with Diane. She is living in her own apartment now over on Wadsworth. Let me give you her number."

I called and told Diane I was back in town. We made arrangements to have coffee the next day. We talked for hours, catching up on each other's lives, what we had been doing since we last saw each other. It was here that the Universe stepped in guiding me to take the correct fork in the road.

"I've been working at Children's Hospital; in the Pediatric Intensive Care Unit. You know the PICU. It is great. I have learned so much there. Working with all those kids, seeing them get better and go back to their families is the best reward" Diane said with such enthusiasm. "I know how much you wanted to work with kids too. You wanted to work at Children's if I remember right" she continued. "Why don't you put in an application. I'm sure with your experience they would hire you in a minute. Here's the name and number of the person you need to call. Maybe we can work together. Wouldn't that be fun? Just like the old days in school" she concluded.

Mom was pretty much back on her feet by the end of May and I was running out of money. I found the phone number that Diane had given me and called.

"Can you come for an interview tomorrow?" they asked.

"Yes" I said. "What time should I be there? 9:00? Great. I will see you then."

Although it would take me only 40 minutes to drive to Children's, I left an hour and a half early. I thought I would give myself some extra time in case I got lost; downtown had changed so much since I had left six years ago. And since that is where I had lent my energy, I did get lost;

arriving only 10 minutes before my interview was to start.

I met with the nursing supervisor. She reviewed my application and asked me several of the usual questions, "Why do you want to work here? What do you think you can contribute?"

After the interview was over she said "I think you will fit in well here. We have positions in the Pediatric and Newborn ICU's. Which would you like to work in?"

I started to panic. Spontaneity is not one of my strong suits. "It would be great to work with Diane in the PICU" I said to myself. "But I really want to work with the babies. I don't know which one to chose."

"Babies. I want to work with the babies" came out of my mouth before my brain had even decided on those words.

"Good" the supervisor said. "I'll take you on a tour of the unit. You can start July 28th. Will that be okay?"

I walked out of the building and rejoiced. I was once again gainfully employed; at the hospital I had been dreaming about for four years. I was unaware of how important a decision I had just made. For the people I was to meet here in the NICU would be my guides to the Puzzle Master.

After that day I saw Diane only once. She disappeared from my life as quickly as she had appeared. Angels stay only as long as they are needed.

Chapter 6

A Guide Named Sue

Of course being new, there was orientation to the unit and care of the newborn. This consisted of classes in pathophysiology of the newborn and premature infant, how to run the breathing machines, how to use all the equipment which was far different than what I had used before. We took care of the babies with instructors standing by our side for the first two months, as much for our safety as the babies. In all, orientation lasted three months. Then we were on our own.

I was placed on nights, which is where everyone seemed to start. We worked 10 hour shifts then; 10:00pm until 8:00am. The 34 bed NICU was divided into two teams, Red and Green. And of course there were openings on both teams but I was *assigned* to the Red Team.

Sue was in charge of the Red Team as well as my

supervisor. She was about my same age, 25, at that time. Sue was a social butterfly; cute, petite, and of course blonde. She could party with the best of them. Yet she ruled the unit with an iron fist. She would not tolerate mistakes.

For reasons unknown to me at the time; she took my friend Dee and I under her wing. She gave us the most difficult assignments. She would quiz us on pathophysiology until we knew it backwards and forwards. We were being groomed to be the "star" nurses of the unit.

Sue was not one to show emotion, at least not in front of her staff. One night a set of twins were admitted. Three hours later one of the twins had bleeding in his brain. It was obvious to all of us that he would not survive the night.

I found Sue in the bathroom crying, something I had not seen her do before. She looked at me, embarrassed for having been caught. We talked awhile until the tears stopped. That night a bond was formed, we became more than supervisor and staff, we became friends.

We started going out socially. At first it was just for drinks and fun. The entire night shift would go to Elly Mae's for breakfast. It was the restaurant of choice since they would actually serve us drinks at 8:00am. As time progressed and we spent more time together, I found that there was a much deeper aspect to Sue. An aspect I never imagined.

Sue introduced me to Leo, her friend and mentor. Leo was a stereotypical hippie from the 60's and looked like the picture next to guru in the dictionary. He had a long white beard which he had not trimmed since 1965 and a long white pony tail to match. And his cologne of choice more times than not was "Au de Pot."

Yet he was a very wise man. He talked of a world that I

did not know existed; a world of energy and "qi"; a world of metaphysics.

It fascinated me. He assigned us books like *Siddhartha, Toa Te Ching*, and *The Egyptian Book of the Dead* to read. Books that stimulated my brain, my imagination. Books that sparked some deep inner knowing that I could not identify. After reading said books, Sue and I would discuss them over dinner. Leo taught us how to play with this energy, this qi. Sue and I found ourselves spending hours making the plastic seagull hanging from her ceiling spin around, first in one direction then the other. It was a world we talked about only to each other for fear of being labeled "freak."

It was a side trip that I had to take. It was a world that I had to discover; or rediscover if you ask the Puzzle Master. The Universal push toward "babies" had lead me to the perfect guides. How different the path would look now had I said Pediatric Intensive Care instead of "babies" at that most important fork in my journey.

Chapter 7

Another Step Closer

Sue's relentless pursuit of our perfection as staff nurses paid high dividends. Dee and I achieved Level III status, the highest possible level for a staff nurse, in record time. And because of this Dee and I were prepared when the opportunity arose to become Neonatal Nurse Practitioners.

Practitioners function in dual disciplines, medicine as well as nursing. It would involve another year of intensive study. It was as intense as any medical school. After that year and a year of internship; we would be able to diagnose, prescribe medication, interpret x-rays and manage the breathing machines. The only thing we didn't do was surgery.

After practitioner school, I chose to work on the Flight Team. The team consisted of a practitioner, a respiratory therapist and an emergency medical technician. We would travel by ambulance, plane or helicopter with our two tackle boxes full of equipment to community hospitals which did not have the level of care that Children's had.

Often times, after we had made our plan of treatment, there was still several hours of time before we reached our destination. It was during these times that we would just talk to each other. More times than not we spent more time with each other than with our families; as it was not uncommon for transports to last 10 to 12 hours.

Erica was a respiratory therapist and one of my team mates. She was into exercise and was always trying to get me to come to the gym with her. "I have a great coach" she would say. "I can get guest passes for you. I bet he could help you a lot. You'll see. All those endorphins make you feel great. You'll never want to stop."

"Thanks for the offer. I really appreciate the gesture. Maybe some other time though" I would tell her. You would think she would get the message after three months of trying.

One evening as we were flying to Wyoming I gazed out the plane window. The sunset was spectacular. "Such a great night" I said. "To think that we are able to witness this God sent sunset. How many people do you think are unaware that it is even here tonight?" I asked Erica.

She said nothing for several minutes. She just looked at me with this curious smile on her face. I smiled back and simply continued to enjoy the sunset in silence, in my own world. About ten minutes later she broke the silence.

"You should come to my church. Well it really isn't a church, not in the traditional sense. It doesn't have stained glass windows or pews or even a Jesus on the cross in front. It's more spiritual than religious. Mary Beth is the preacher. I think you would like it a lot."

For the next several weeks she hounded me every time I saw her. "You should come" she would always end the shift with. More to make her quit bugging me than anything else I agreed to go.

"I'll come this Sunday" I told her. "Will that satisfy you?"

"Yes. I'll see you there."

It was indeed a "different" type of church. To see it from the outside one would never know a church existed inside; it was just an ordinary building. The congregation sat in folding chairs in rows. They were purposely uncomfortable I think so we wouldn't fall asleep during the sermon. The pulpit was a simple wooden lectern. Mary Beth; the preacher; wore not robes but a simple Sunday dress.

When she began to speak it reminded me of my sessions with Sue and Leo. She spoke of spirituality but not religious dogma. I felt as if I were home once again.

After attending for several Sundays I decided I wanted to become an official member of the church. I signed the card and made it official. The next Sunday they welcomed me as a full member of the church.

The very next Sunday Erica approached me. "I just wanted to let you know I am quitting the transport team. I'm going back to be a staff therapist. And I am also quitting the church."

"Quitting" I said with surprise. "I thought you loved it here?"

"Not anymore. I'm going to a different church."

I never saw Erica again. It confused me for several months. I couldn't understand why she was so adamant about my coming; why she left so abruptly?

It wasn't until several months later and in retrospect that I received my answer. Erica had guided me to the precise location where I was to meet my final human angel guide; the one who would lead me to the Puzzle Master herself.

Chapter 8

The Final Leg

This final angel came disguised as a young woman named Sue. I noticed her standing in the background at church one Sunday. She appeared very shy; standing alone, hands folded in front of her, looking mostly at the floor. She looked as if anyone were to actually speak to her she would have a panic attack or a heart attack and die right there on the spot.

I knew exactly how she felt. For I too was shy, unable to speak to strangers. I gathered all my courage and walked up to her. "Hi. My name is Ann. Welcome," I said as sweat began to pour down my face. She nodded her head in acknowledgement but never spoke. It would be two months before I ever heard her voice.

Over the next year Sue began to open up and talk. We attended several classes together at the church and became friends. The common bond of our shyness seemed to help us bond. We encouraged each other to talk. We praised each other when we did. Together we helped each other step out of our boxes, even though it was just a step or two.

Over that year the congregation ebbed and flowed. Some months there would be 50 people, the next there would be only 20 or so. By the end of that year the count was down to 10; Sue and I among them. We decided as a group that we no longer needed the big room we called church. And it was next to impossible for the ten of us to supply enough money to pay the rent. So in order to save money and to keep the church going we moved our meetings to Mary Beth's house.

It was a more intimate setting and we came to know each other better. We found out that Sue had recently lost both her parents. She felt alone. Her only brother lived out of state. She now considered us her family.

That year for Christmas Sue arranged a private session for the 7 women in the group. Afterwards she invited us to her house for lunch. We munched on chips and salsa while we talked. Later we dined on fabulous garlic chicken and salad. At the end of this beautiful day we all thanked her for the yoga experience. Each one of us commented on how much more relaxed we felt.

Sue then brought out some pamphlets. Interestingly enough they were not about yoga at all. "Here" she said. "This is the chiropractor and acupuncturist I go to. Both of them are really great." She looked mainly at me and continued "I bet she could help you with your knees. She can do amazing things."

"I've been thinking about going to an acupuncturist" I said. "You say she is really good? Maybe I'll call her and make an appointment soon."

I folded it in half and stuffed the brochure in my purse and didn't think much more about it. Sue continued to ask me almost weekly if I had called to make an appointment yet. "No, but soon" was always my response.

I had taken the pamphlet out of my purse and placed it on my desk. There it waited patiently amongst bills and junk mail for me to find it once again. Several months later as I was finally filing the papers which now obscured the desk top, I found the flyer.

"I should really call her" I muttered to myself. But instead of calling, I placed it back on the desk. It was now out of sight, out of mind once again. Yet it was still in the loop of Universal Synchronicity.

Chapter 9

The Blessing

In April of that year we had a spring snow storm. The ground and roads were covered in snow and ice. The trees were just beginning to show their first leaves. The heavy snow caused limbs to break and cover the ground as if an atomic bomb had gone off.

As was my usual routine, I stopped to get coffee on my way to work. The sidewalk in front of the coffee shop had been shoveled, but the constant freezing and melting of the snow left it icy this time of the night. I managed to make my way in without incident. I came there so often they knew my order by heart; a triple vente, nonfat, no whip mocha.

I was out the door in less than five minutes. As I was pressing my key chain to open my car door I found myself embracing the sidewalk. Now sprawled on the sidewalk I found I still had my cup of coffee intact in my hand. “Thank God” I thought “This is a $4 cup of coffee.” I gathered my wits about me and tried to sit up. There was now a searing sharp pain in my left ankle. I was sure I had broken it. I grabbed it with my left hand and felt no bones sticking out, at least that was a good sign. I hoped that pressure and sheer will would make the pain stop, but it continued.

“I’ll be late for work,” I said as I watched my breath turn into a cloud of steam. I gathered myself together, awkwardly arose from the ground trying not to spill the coffee I had sacrificed my ankle for, and began to walk to the car. It hurt to put any pressure on it so I hopped the last few remaining steps. I drove to the hospital and parked in the garage. Never before had the walk into the hospital seemed so long or painful.

It must have taken me ten minutes to limp and hop the hundred yards or so to the ICU. As I walked in the door huffing and puffing Donna, the day shift practitioner asked “What happened to you? Your pants are all wet and muddy. Why are you limping?”

My ankle had hurt so bad I didn’t even notice that the outside of my pant leg as soaked and covered in mud. “I fell” I confessed. “And it really hurts.”

“Well I’m taking you to the emergency room. And I’m not taking no for an answer. Two hours and three x-rays later I had my ankle tucked inside a most attractive black boot with Velcro accent straps. It wasn’t Jimmy Choo; it wasn’t even Wal-Mart but at least black goes with everything.

“Not broken” the doctor said. “Just badly sprained. Keep the boot on until it quits hurting.”

For three weeks I walked around in that boot. My ankle

still hurt almost as bad as the day I did it. I was beginning to think that it would be this way forever.

I was cleaning my desk top once again. I gathered up the no longer needed papers from their resting place to take to the trash, and as I was heading towards the final resting place of all such "frivolous" items, a single piece of paper floated to the ground from the stack. It was the pamphlet from the acupuncturist! I picked it up and read it once again. That all knowing voice in my head said "Call. What do you have to lose? You might even gain something"

Down the stairs my boot and I limped and finally placed the call. "I need to make an appointment. Wednesday at 2:00 pm is okay. Thank you."

Chapter 10

Destiny Found

To observe this moment in isolation; to the casual observer; this would appear to be a random encounter. The recommendation of a friend; a phone number on the bottom of a brochure; my only connection to this unknown woman.

Yet when one steps back and observes the totality of the path, beyond this single moment in time, one can see there is no randomness in the Universe. There are no accidents. Never could I alone have devised such an intricate, detailed and precisely timed plan. For only the Universe could have coordinated the "chance" encounters which led us to each other. The meeting of our Spirits was a result of this Universal Synchronicity. The Universe had been guiding us together for most of our lifetime.

The brochure which would not leave my possession,

was the final link, final connection required for our meeting. Its appearance in my life was the result of dozens of Earth Guides and Earth Angels guiding me along the path so perfectly constructed by the Universe. I am thankful and grateful to each and every one for their guidance.

It was a phone call that would change my life forever. For on the other end of the phone was the Puzzle Master and I was about to meet her at long last. The quest to find her had ended, but the journey of healing was just beginning.

Part 2

The Path of the Puzzle Master

Chapter 11

The Beginning

The Puzzle Master blessed the planet with her arrival on September 8, 1964; a full 10 years and 364 days after my arrival. She was born into a loving family with two parents and two older siblings; twins; a brother and sister. From this moment on she would be known to the world as Shawna.

Shawna grew up in Indian Hills in Colorado. As the name suggests it had the terrain of a Daniel Boone adventure with pine trees, meadows and wild flowers. She had horses to ride. Deer, fox and coyote shared their home with her. All of nature was her back yard. She could think of no better place to live, except maybe the ocean.

Even at an early age Shawna showed the talents and gifts of a Healer. By the age of seven or eight she was giving massages to anyone who would sit still long enough. She started with her mom and dad, giving them "back rubs" when they came home from work. By the time she was twelve she gave the best back rubs in Jefferson County.

Her mom; Pat; used to work as a police dispatcher. Shawna didn't like to be away from her mom at that time. And since they lived only a few blocks from the police station; many afternoons when Shawna wanted company she would simply walk or ride her bike down to visit her mom. She would offer to give back rubs to anyone who needed or wanted them. She thought perhaps this way no one would be opposed to a twelve year old hanging out at the police station.

Everyone would comment on what a great job she did. Always they felt better afterwards. People always commented about the warmth, the heat which came to them through her hands. Even as a child the Healer within her was already apparent. It's just at that age, she had no name for it.

Shawna also became familiar with massage, acupuncture and chiropractors from the patient's perspective. When she was seventeen she had an auto accident. She was driving east bound on Hampton Avenue and hit a patch of ice. The car began to slide as she headed for the concrete barriers which separated the left and right sides of the road. A voice loud and clear said "Take your hands off the wheel!" She let go of the wheel and the car was "steered" through a small opening between the barriers; just large enough for the car to fit through at only one precise angle. The car rolled over into a ravine, landing right side up. She had severe whiplash but was otherwise unharmed.

She had severe headaches after the accident. Every

morning she awoke with a migraine. Her mom took her to a chiropractor who had a massage therapist in his office. It helped her pain, her healing. It was an experience, a memory which would guide her down a path she was as yet unaware.

Chapter 12

The Destruction

Immediately after finishing high school, Shawna married the man she had been dating throughout junior and senior high school. He was a very controlling, manipulative man. He controlled Shawna's every move, thought and feeling for many years.

Bob was very good at what he did. He could convince you that the sky was green when you knew it was blue. Shawna's parents were among the few who were able to see through Bob's façade. They begged her not to marry him. They took her to counseling in hopes that a therapist could show her the error of her decision.

After all the facts, mostly negative, were presented to her the therapist and her parents asked, "Do you still want to marry him? Do you really want to live this kind of life with him?"

It was the Healer in her which gave this answer, "Yes. I know I can help him."

It was a battle she fought for 17 years; through several years of dating and 14 years of marriage, but could not win. Not only could she not help him, he tried and almost succeeded in destroying her; her Heart, her Soul, her very Spirit.

Through out most of their marriage Bob did not hold a steady job. He always had excuses for why they didn't work out and never did he take ownership for their failure. It was always "Those people are just ass holes. I can't work with them" Or "This just isn't the job for me." Or "If I was a Mexican or Black they'd hire me. Its 'cause I'm white I can't find a job. Damn Mexicans."

In reality he was lying, cheating and stealing from everyone, in every job. Bill; Shawna's dad; had tried to get Bob a job at the Fire Station where he worked. It was a "ride-along" program which would lead to permanent employment. Several months later Bill was asked by his coworkers to tell Bob to leave and never come back. He had stolen money from them; more than once. Bill never told Shawna of the incident, trying to protect her. This was not an isolated incident. The list would continue to grow for many years.

Although Bob told Shawna he loved her; he beat her Spirit, her Soul, her very Heart into the ground. Since high school he would always say, "No one will ever love you but me." After years of having this engraved upon her Soul, she believed him. It was one of the reasons she stayed so long; that and the love of her sons. Her sons that were and always would be her whole world.

Bob would also tell her how to think, how to feel. She was not "allowed" to have her own opinions, her own wishes and dreams. It was always about "him," his desires, his wants and needs.

Even in regards to "love making", the most intimate act between a man and a woman, she was never good enough. He would always talk about other women and how much he desired them. He would watch porn while "making love" to her. He would project himself into the movie. It seemed there was always more than just the two of them present during these times. On one or two occasions, when Shawna gathered all her courage that she could muster; when she could cope no longer with the situation, she would try to voice her concern. She would try to tell him how much this hurt her, how degraded she felt. His answer was always the same, "So you think I'm an asshole, don't you. Just remember no one will ever love you but me. If you don't want to be alone forever then deal with it." Each time he spoke these words to her; her feelings, her concerns, her very being was negated.

That fear of being alone; of never being loved again, kept her in her marriage for 14 years. She learned to keep quite. And the essence of Shawna began to disappear.

Chapter 13

The Healer Awakens

Shawna had thought about leaving Bob on more than one occasion. Each time the fear overtook her. The thought that she would hurt Bob in any way; or her sons was more than she could bare. It was worse than the pain of staying.

Each night while the rest of her family slept, Shawna prayed to God through sometimes not so silent tears; "Please God show me the way. I am willing to do the work I have to do, but I need your guidance. Please show me the way or take me home. I can't live like this any longer." On a cold snowy morning in December God answered Shawna's prayer.

As was her usual routine, after she got her oldest son off to school, she fed the youngest. She sipped her coffee as she watched him try to feed himself oatmeal. It made her smile to just look at him; for he was the love of her life and the center of her world. As with most kids his age, he absorbed more through his ears and head than his mouth. Shawna bathed him and dressed him in little toddler jeans and a long sleeve shirt then sent him off to play.

She caught a glimpse of herself as she passed the mirror in the hall. She noticed that she had oatmeal in her hair and on her face. It made her laugh again. "I guess a bath is in order for me too" she told her son as he played. "Mommy will be right back. You play nice while I'm gone."

Shawna always welcomed the warmth of a hot shower, especially on these cold winter mornings. She was lost in thought as the bathroom filled with steam. As she stepped into the shower and as the water ran over her she once again prayed, "God please give me guidance. Show me the way."

Emerging from the shower she wrapped herself in a large towel and took another from the rack and began to dry her hair. Shawna glanced into the now foggy mirror. She stopped immediately and took a step backwards. For there written on the mirror in perfect penmanship was the word "MASSAGE." She said the word out loud and it resonated with every cell of her body. The Healer hidden within her for all these years began to awaken. It was the guidance she had been looking for. All she could do was cry and give thanks to God. At last she was excited to be alive.

Chapter 14

Healer Reborn

That evening as Bob was hanging Christmas lights along the back boarder of the house, Shawna gathered all her strength and approached him. She had been thinking, analyzing, processing this guidance from God. She knew that just asking to go to school would not be an option. Bob had not finished high school. He was expelled his senior year and told never to come back, ever! He had no desire to further his education and he did not think his wife needed more education either.

Shawna gathered all the courage and determination she possessed. For once she was going to tell Bob exactly how she felt for now she had direction. With divine guidance on her side giving her courage she walked up to him and said "Bob, I want out of this marriage. I want a divorce. I haven't been happy for a very long time. I am not fulfilled in any way shape or form. I even missed out on college because I married you. I can't take this any more. I want out! I want to go back to school."

Shawna knew that he could turn on a dime, one moment he was calm, quiet; the next moment he would be literally raging at her.

She stood by bracing herself for his wrath. This time Shawna was determined to stand her ground. Bob hesitated; Christmas lights still in his hand; then slowly stepped down from the ladder and looked at Shawna. The words which came from his mouth shocked her. "Well what school do you want to go to? Just tell me. I promise to be better. I promise to be a better husband. You name it. You just can't leave me."

Still not quite sure of his response Shawna said "I want to go to massage school."

"Okay then, massage school it is," Bob replied.

Bob did not miss a step. It was if the promise he made only moments ago never came from his mouth. Once again he took control of her life. It was *he* who found and approved a massage school for her to attend. She was not "allowed" to attend just any school. He even went so far as to get a friend of both of theirs to enroll with her. Shawna was glad for the company; for someone to be a study partner. Yet she wondered deep in her heart if Bob was using this friend as his own personal spy. It would only be in the future that she would learn to trust those feelings in her heart; for they were true.

Shawna excelled in school. It was her sanctuary; she was learning new things, a new philosophy, and she was having new experiences. The best part was she was meeting new people, healers like herself. Shawna now had people of like mind with which she could converse about her experiences.

As the last part of her schooling Shawna had to do an internship. This meant she had to find a place where she could further perfect her talent by giving free massages; clinicals was the official name . Bob would not hear of her going to look for a position herself. He came home from work one day and said "I found you a job." Shawna asked where. He replied "With Dr. Jim's office. You know the little league football team's chiropractor."

Divine intervention had lead Shawna to massage school. Only in retrospect would she be able to see that Bob's instance on "finding her a job" was part of the divine Universal Synchronicity of her path. It was guiding her to all that she had hoped for; had wished for; yet she would have to conquer a great dark abyss before her dreams would be brought into reality.

Chapter 15

Bliss among the Ruins

Shawna reported to work the next day. This was actually the second time she had met Dr. Jim. The first time was two years before when her son sprained his ankle playing football. Bob and Shawna had brought him to see Dr. Jim, the team Doctor.

The moment Shawna saw him, she fell into total lust with him. She thought he was the most attractive, vibrant, sexy man on the face of the earth. There was also something in the way he carried himself. She watched as he greeted patients; he shook hands and gave hugs to men as well as women. It was not hard to see that he had a genuine kind and caring soul.

Jim had tended to her son's ankle and she did not see him again; until today. She had forgotten how beautiful he was. This time when their eyes met he gave her the hint of a smile. “Here to work?” he asked.

“Yes” was all she could say around the lump in her throat.

Jim showed her to her room and then left. She set up her massage table and waited patiently for clients to arrive. It didn’t take long. Since the massage was part of her training and therefore free, Jim would send as many clients her way as possible. Each client got a fifteen minute massage. It was short but very effective.

Shawna was already very good at what she did. The Healer inside of her was blossoming once again. Every client raved about her massages. They asked if she was going to stay permanently. Jim said “It might be a possibility. We could use a good massage therapist in the office. We’ll talk after school is over.” Shawna was floating on cloud nine; not only would she be working with Jim, but doing that which she loved; Healing.

There was no doubt in Jim’s mind that he would hire her after her internship. She was very, very good at what she did. And there was a chemistry between the two of them like no other they had ever known.

Jim did hire her as a full time massage therapist. As time went on her practice grew. There was hardly a day when her schedule was not full. Her clients loved her and often she would find more than her usual $40 waiting for her at the end of a session.

Shawna had a divine connection with the Universe. There were times that she just “knew” which muscles to work, how to massage them, sometimes in ways that were not taught in any book. And on rare occasions which were becoming more frequent; it felt as if her hands were not her own. They felt so large, more than twice their normal size. And they would feel so warm; as if heated by the sun. It was at these times that Shawna knew that God, the Angels, and the Guides had taken over.

These experiences were not something she could talk to Bob about. He wasn't very interested in what she was doing or learning. One other factor prevented Shawna from talking to Bob; he didn't believe in God in any way shape or form. She had tried in the past to talk to him about these occurrences. He would only call her "freak" and then walk away, shaking his head.

Shawna found an ally in Jim. As "luck" would have it the office closed between noon and three for lunch. It was during these times that Shawna and Jim would talk. Never once did he call her a freak; and he actually listened to what she said. He talked to her, not at her. He never told her how to think or feel or be. Soon they were talking about other things as well. There was small talk but eventually they talked about their marriages which were not working out, for either of them. In essence both their marriages had been over for many years; yet neither had the courage to leave yet. They talked of dreams they had and goals they wanted to accomplish in their lives.

The more they talked, the more they found they had in common. Shawna and Jim's love grew within those three hour blocks of time they shared each day. Sometimes they would go to the gym and workout. Sometimes they would meet somewhere and spend time in the mountains; eating lunch and talking. And yes, sometimes they made passionate love. The only thing which seemed askew was the timing; for neither was divorced yet. Sometimes love; especially true love; has no respect for the man made invention of time.

Shawna and Jim tried several times to break off their relationship but they always found their way back to each other. Shawna especially felt the guilt. She no longer loved Bob but did not want to hurt him or the children. It was the Healer in her, the very essence of her Heart and Soul which said "Cause no pain, cause no harm." She was torn between a man she now loved deeply, a man who was destroying her, and her sons. The sons that were her whole world and always would be.

They did not tell anyone of their love, not because they were ashamed, but because they didn't want to hurt any of the other parties involved. Shawna was healing, growing strong with Jim's love, yet she was still not strong enough to leave Bob. In time, as she grew stronger, she and Jim planned to divorce their respective spouses. Then they would be able to declare their love for each other openly. Perhaps they would even marry.

The Universe was working on a different time table than Shawna and Jim. It was as if God and the Universe said, "Shawna you need to leave now. You need to leave before your Heart, your Soul, your very Spirit is destroyed forever. You are strong enough." With that, the Universe set the wheels in motion. There are no accidents.

Shawna and Jim were both working, healing patients in their own special way. They both heard shouting, screaming, coming from the waiting room and went running. They almost ran into each other as they came to a sudden halt.

There standing in the lobby was Bob and Jim's wife Sheila. With his lies and manipulations of the truth he had recruited Sheila into his "army;" an army with a single mission, to destroy Shawna's Heart and Soul. Bob was pounding his fist on the desk, screaming so that the whole building could hear him, "Where is that son of a bitch Jim? And where is Shawna? I want to talk to them NOW!"

As Shawna and Jim approached the desk Bob screamed, "Are you two having an affair?"

They had to be honest and said, "Yes." The proverbial cat was now out of the bag. Shawna was about to fall into the darkest abyss of her life.

Bob was not kind during the divorce. He was as controlling, manipulative and deceitful during this time as he was during the marriage. He was out to win for himself; to destroy Shawna at any cost. Bob launched his attack at her most vulnerable area; the area he knew would wound, would hurt her most; her children.

No tactic, no strategy was beneath him. He began by kicking Shawna out of the house. "You had the affair so you leave. Pack your things and get out." The fact that he had numerous affairs during their marriage did not seem a factor. "After all" he would tell her "if you gave me what I needed I wouldn't have to go looking else where."

He went so far as to tap into Shawna and Jim's private phones. Bob would then splice together conversations. He was very good at what he did and could manipulate and transform the words to his advantage. Bob would then play these doctored tapes for his sons. "See, here is the proof that your mother abandoned you."

Shawna tried to tell her sons the truth, that she loved them more than life itself. She would try to call them at night but Bob would tell her "They don't want to talk to you" and would hang up. He would call her at night and say "The boys are going to bed. Don't you miss reading them bedtime stories?" Bob would then laugh and once again hang up the phone before she could even answer. He fed the boys lies and manipulated their minds. It was the only way he could win the war; destroy Shawna's world and her relationship with her boys; for the truth was 360 degrees in the opposite direction.

She cried every night over the loss of her children, for the loss of their love. The loss, the pain so devastating she no longer wanted to live. Her whole world had been destroyed. Her heart so wounded, so broken, she thought it would never heal. Shawna was sure she would die from this broken Heart.

Chapter 16

Turmoil

Turmoil was the only word to describe Shawna's life. She was going through a bitter divorce with Bob. Her sons, the center of her world were withdrawing their love from her. Yet she was experiencing true love for the first time as her relationship with Jim continued to grow. Her plate was as full as if she was seated at a Thanksgiving feast. All this and she was about to embark on a new adventure; Chinese Medical School.

Shawna had been a massage therapist for now ten years. It was the most rewarding work she had ever done. The ability to help others, to place her hands; which were often not her own, on another and watch them heal made her heart sing. She rejoiced at being the vessel through which God worked. But the years of constant work had taken their toll physically. Her hands could no longer serve, the pain growing intense each time she massaged tight muscles.

Once again she asked God to "Please show me the way. Show me the path." And just as He had answered her so long ago in the shower, He answered once again. This time in the form of a dinner guest.

Shawna and Jim were riding in the car with friends; on the way to the Lowe's building downtown for dinner. The usual small talk filled the time as they rode. And of course the question of "What do you do?" was asked of Shawna. She told their guest of her work as a massage therapist. Of how over time her hands could no longer take the stress, the constant manipulation of tight muscles. She told of the pain she now experienced and how she would have to give up her passion of massage. Shawna shared how the Healer in her was lost now, looking for a new path.

God answered her through this human angel disguised as a dinner guest that night. "Have you ever thought about acupuncture?" she asked. That answered resonated with every cell in Shawna's body. She went looking for a Chinese Medicine School the next day.

Shawna was unsure of how she would accomplish this new goal, this new adventure in healing. She was essentially homeless. Since Bob had kicked her out of the house she had no permanent home of her own. She carried her few worldly belongings in her car. She would spend the night with a friend here, a friend there. Sometimes she would stay with her sister or her parents.

Yet she never stayed in one place too long, afraid she would wear out her welcome. But she had faith. If this was the right thing to do, God would provide.

From the very first day of Chinese Medical School, Shawna knew she had found her new Healing profession, her new passion. Although it was difficult at times; learning a new healing philosophy, all the herbal remedies, and the hundreds of acupuncture points; filled Shawna with an inner joy.

Among the classes she could pursue was a course entitled "5 Element Acupuncture." The course description spoke of the five elements; water, wood, fire, earth, and metal. It spoke of learning to balance the elements through special 5 element points. The description continued with what a beautiful and effective form of healing this was. But it would be added courses, added class time mainly on weekends, added clinical time. She did not have the time, energy or money to pursue this course.

Many of her classmates enrolled in this course by the second semester of school. They told Shawna of its beauty and special healing quality. They encouraged her every semester to "Start now, please Shawna. Not only will it add to your Healing ability, it will help *you* heal as well;" for they all knew of her "woundedness."

Shawna continued with only the basic classes which were hard enough to handle especially when she was basically homeless, living in her car. There were other "personal" hurdles which she also had to contend with; there was the ongoing divorce, the loss of her children, and her father's illness.

During this time Shawna also had the added heartache of her father's illness. He had emphysema; brought on by years of inhaling smoke from the fires he fought and his two pack a day habit of cigarettes. He was on oxygen at home and in constant pain, unable to breathe.

Bill was her rock, her support. He was always there for her. Her dad would always tell her "Bob should be glad I can't get to him because you know I would kill the son of a bitch for what he has done to you and the kids." Shawna knew that her dad was telling the truth. Secretly she was glad he couldn't leave the mountain, he wouldn't do well in jail.

His health continued to fail and he was in excruciating pain. Every breath was a struggle. Everyone in the family knew it would not be long, including her dad. On a cool April afternoon, while talking to her mom on the phone, she heard a bang. "Call 911!" her mom shouted into the phone.

Bill had ended his pain, his agony, there on the deck in the mountains he loved so much. Every one was devastated, Shawna the most. For she was "Daddy's little girl." He had been her strength, her rock, her loving light in the darkness of the abyss.

She felt her Heart break. How would she ever survive without him; she loved him so.

Chapter 17

Reconstruction

Now both legally divorced, Jim and Shawna were free to fan their ember of love into a full fledged bon fire. It was a blaze the likes of which Shawna had never seen or experienced before.

For the first time in her life, she was loved the way a woman should be loved; totally, completely, respectfully. There were no "third parties" in this relationship; for Jim loved her and her *alone.* Jim held her Heart in his hands and applied his magic loving salve. Slowly, ever so slowly her wounds quit bleeding and they began to heal.

He loved her and only her. "You are the complete package babe" he would tell her. He allowed her to have her own opinions, her own thoughts and feelings. Jim never judged one thought, one action. He talked to her not at her. They made plans together, they set goals together. And unlike Bob, Jim was willing to work to accomplish those goals.

With his love, Jim was able to save the foundation, the essence, the "Who" that was Shawna. He bulldozed down the house of *lies* that Bob had built there. He replaced that hou*se of lies* with bricks of love and joy, respect and honor, and truth. Now sitting on that foundation was the mansion that belonged there, "Shawna."

Shawna had joy in her life again. She went skiing for the first time since she was fifteen. Bob didn't like the cold so she gave up that passion to please him. But with Jim, even the simplest of things; like sitting on the floor at Barnes and Noble reading books or listening to music brought her joy; because that is what they now brought to the experience; joy and love. The only thing missing from these moments was the love of her sons.

Her classmates continued to encourage her to take the 5 Element course. Every semester it was the same, "Oh Shawna, this is so great. Please sign up now before it is too late." At every request she replied "I can't. Not now. I just can't add any more to my plate right now." And so they watched as she sunk deeper and deeper into the abyss. For although she had the love of Jim, she did not have the love of her children and it was destroying her inside.

At the end of her third of four years of Chinese Medical School Shawna and Jim did get married. On Memorial Day weekend on a sunny beach in Mexico surrounded by a few intimate friends and family. She had only two regrets that day; that her dad was there only in Spirit to see her wed the man of her dreams, and that her children were not there. Both broke her Heart. The abyss was getting deeper and darker with each passing day.

There were periods of uncontrollable crying. A deep

dark depression set in. She thought of suicide often when in this dark abyss. The guilt of the affair before she was divorced, the hurt she felt she caused to Bob and the children mixed with the love of this incredible man Jim, was more than she could endure.

Yet she thought she could handle it on her own. "I can get through this myself!" she would tell herself. Phone calls in the middle of the night with only sobbing on the other end told her friends and loved ones that she needed help. Each time they would rush to her side thinking this may be the end, only to find her curled in a fetal position sobbing uncontrollably in a corner of the kitchen.

Shawna's friends from Acupuncture School, especially her "study buddy" Brian kept telling her of this wonderful specialized form of acupuncture called 5 Element Acupuncture. Unlike traditional acupuncture it was more than just "Where does it hurt" and then applying needles. They encouraged her to learn this new form of acupuncture, for in the learning she had to experience it as well.

It was a blessing and a curse to Shawna that Jim had two children of his own. Every other weekend they would come to stay with them. They accepted Shawna with every ounce of their being. They wanted to snuggle with her, have her read them stories. It only reminded Shawna of the loss of her own children. She would run to her room, shut the door and cry uncontrollably; unable to bear even the sound of a child's voice.

Often times she would plan weekend adventures and outings with her friends on the weekends the kids stayed. Anything so that she would not have to deal with them. Anything to not be reminded that her own children had been ripped from her Heart by Bob's manipulation and deceit. With the center of her Universe gone, she began to implode.

Her friends could stand by no longer. They could not watch her fall unabated into the abyss, into this darkness of depression. An intervention of sorts was needed. Brian, in a way that only he could persuade her said "At least try a treatment. You never know, it might help."

"Alright" she said. "I'll try one." That very instant Brian picked up the phone and made her an appointment.

Five Element acupuncture was like nothing else Shawna had ever experienced. It treated the whole of the body. The physical, spiritual, mental and emotional aspects of life were all treated with equal reverence. She learned how the elements; water, wood, fire, earth and metal; all worked in harmony with each other. How if one is out of balance it affects the entire body.

It was a beautiful form of acupuncture; a beautiful form of Healing. It even had beautiful point names such as The Gate to Heaven, Essence Tower and Spirit Seal.

Much to her amazement, Shawna felt much better after her initial treatment. So much so that she continued with weekly sessions for many months. At last she was beginning to heal. She could feel her Heart, her Soul, her Spirit begin to come alive once again.

She fell in love with the sheer beauty with which it could heal. "This is the way I want to help Heal people," she said with tears in her eyes. "With this beautiful modality which has changed my life forever."

At last she was ready to pursue 5 Element Acupuncture, both as a way to heal herself and others. Jim encouraged her through out her classes in Chinese Medicine School and Acupuncture. "You can do this babe. You are so smart and intelligent" he would tell her on the days she just knew she couldn't make it any farther. How very different was this man than the one she left.

Shawna did find the energy, the time, and the money to become certified in 5 Element Acupuncture. And she continued to heal herself, to become whole once again. The essence of Shawna began to returned.

The day Shawna graduated from 5 Element Acupuncture School the world received a great gift, that of a Healer Extraordinaire. Shawna was a Wounded Healer, but there is no better Healer than this. For who better to guide ones healing than one who has been to the abyss, survived and themselves healed. It is a testament to the power, the beauty of 5 Element Therapy.

Somehow, someway; with the help of God and the Universe, numerous Earth Angles and the love of a most remarkable man; Shawna survived the turmoil of divorce, the devastating loss of her dad and graduated from Chinese Medical School. It was and is a most amazing accomplishment. Even more so considering the challenges which Shawna endured during this time period.

Chapter 18

The Merging of Paths

Shawna was exhausted after the ordeal of the divorce, the struggle of school for four years and the joy of her wedding. Even though she had worked so hard to become an acupuncturist, she was not yet ready to practice, partly from lack of confidence in her ability. Then again perhaps this was her Universal pause, for we would not meet for another year.

She busied herself with the new home she and Jim had bought. Shawna spent her days painting, plastering, decorating. She wanted it to be perfect. She wanted a home, not just a house for their *lov*e to grow. And grow it did, every single day.

Once the house was finished she was still not ready to "be" an acupuncturist and so she helped Jim in his office. She filed insurance forms, did the books, greeted patients.

Shawna did whatever was needed to make the office run smoothly.

One day in February, at home while they were cuddled in front of the fire Jim said "It's time babe. Its time you started using your acupuncture that you worked so hard for. I'll hire someone to do the office work so don't worry about that. It's time for you to be the Healer that you are."

Shawna looked into his eyes and saw only love. She hugged him as the fire crackled in front of them. "Okay" she said shaking with as much fear as anticipation. "I'll start next week."

Two months later, in April of 2003, she answered the phone in the office. The conversation was brief. "This is Shawna. How can I help you?"

"I need an appointment with the acupuncturist, is that you?"

"Yes. That is me. I can make that appointment for you. How about Wednesday at 2:00? Would that work for you?"

"Yes."

"And your name is?"

"Ann."

"I'll see you Wednesday then. Goodbye."

Chapter 19

A New Beginning

Shawna had wished on more than one occasion that she had never married Bob. To quote a country song she "may have avoided the pain but she would have missed the joy."

For without Bob she would not have had her sons. The sprained ankle of her eldest would have never occurred; she would never have met Jim, the man of her dreams.

It was because of Bob's controlling nature; his insistence that only he could find her a job that she had met Jim once again. That they had the opportunity to fall in love. It was because of Jim's love that she developed the strength and courage to leave Bob.

The seeming tragedy of hands which no longer served in the capacity of massage. An angel disguised as a dinner guest supplying the new way to serve, acupuncture. A deep dark depression, an abyss which lead to the discovery of the beauty and healing capacity of 5 Element Acupuncture.

Tragedies that in retrospect were Blessings and always had been. One must look with a different mind than the one which created the dark cloud to see the silver lining. There are no accidents. There are no coincidences. There is only Universal Synchronicity.

This was the culmination of almost fifty years of Universal Synchronicity. How many twists and turns had our lives taken to reach this point? How many angels had it taken to guide us down this path? If we had changed even one second of our lives, would we have conversed that day? Only God and the Universe know for sure.

Part 3

Journeys of Healing

Chapter 20

Healing can Happen

Even from our very first meeting there was something vaguely familiar about Shawna. It was not the outside shell but what was inside that was most familiar. It was as I call it the "Who." That part of the Soul which doesn't change no matter in what vehicle or lifetime it presents. In Shawna's case it was were the Love, the Light and the Healer within her lived. These were the qualities I recognized from past lifetimes we had shared together.

Yet I was unsure, almost unwilling to believe in my intuitive ability. I was only just beginning to unfold the bud, pedal by pedal. My armor still firmly attached doing its best to "protect" me from harm. I spent countless hours and dollars with other psychics, intuitives; even people who spoke to the Angels. Each one repeated the same phrase,

"You already know this. Why have you come to me?" After seeing six or seven of these individuals, I had to believe that what I "felt and saw" was not illusion.

Not only did our relationship as acupuncturist and patient grow; but our Friendship began to grow as well. The same qualities, the same Who of the Puzzle Master, was also a part of Shawna the Friend. In many ways it became much easier to talk to her, for I was now talking to a Friend as well as a Healer.

We began our Friendship slowly, cautiously; but it did not take long for it to bloom once again. Coffee shared on a sunny afternoon, lunch at the café down the street, a phone conversation was how it began. Little by little she revealed her story to me. It was a tragic story; a story of love lost and now found, of the loss of children through the deceit of their father, of being lost in a dark abyss.

It was also the story of courage, of survival, of rebirth. It was the story of healing. I came to know the woundedness of my Friend and mentor. I developed a trust in her, for I knew she would always guide me with Love, Kindness and no judgment of my life thus far. It gave me courage to know if Shawna survived and healed perhaps I could do the same.

In the rereading of my journeys for this book I have seen that I too have healed. Know that there is a way out of the abyss, out of the darkness. That healing can and will occur no matter when the process begins, no matter if you start at 10 or 20 or 50 as I did. Know that if one can do this, so can all.

Chapter 21

The Meeting of Souls

Although I was excited to finally get pain relief for my ankle, I was scared to death. It was not the acupuncture which scared me; for I knew enough to know that needles as fine as a hair would be placed in my body. I was around needles every day of my life, they represented no fear to me. What scared me was the mere "thought" of having to talk to someone new, a stranger.

By the time I arrive at Shawna's office I was in a cold sweat. I could feel my throat begin to close. No words could escape from beyond the lump which had formed there. I could barely get out "Ann" when the receptionist asked who I was.

I was then handed papers to fill out.They contained the usual array of questions one would fill out at any doctors office; "Why are you here today? If it is an injury, when did it occur? What are your symptoms?" I filled them out and promptly returned them to the receptionist. I now had ten minutes to wait until my appointment.

In those ten minutes I must have ran a thousand scenarios through my head. "I know Sue has told her about me. What if she doesn't like me? What if she thinks I'm a jerk? What if she thinks I'm a freak like others have said? Will she judge me because I am fat?"

My scenarios were interrupted by a voice I barely heard, "Ann?"

"Yes" I said. Only briefly did my eyes glance at the face of the woman standing in front of me before they were once again focused on the carpet at my feet.

"My name is Shawna. Come on back with me and we can get started."

Shaking with fear I rose from the chair. Using the back of her shoes as a guide, I followed her into her room.

The room was not much bigger than a closet. There was just enough room for a massage table and maybe two feet left over to walk around it. The smell of incense filled the room; for reasons I can not explain it made me smile. Even to this day just the smell of Nag Champa brings a smile to my face. Candles supplied the only light in the room. Even on encountering the room for the first time, it had a Sacred feel to it. I knew there was something very special about the combination of this room and the Healer who stood before me.

In the back corner was a single chair. It was this chair that she motioned me to sit in. Shawna then sat cross-legged on the table and began to speak, "Have you ever had acupuncture before?"

I tried to speak but nothing came out. All I could do was shake my head "No."

She gave me a puzzled look but continued, “I do two types of acupuncture, traditional and 5 Element.” She then went on to explain the difference. Shawna told me of the beauty of 5 Element Acupuncture. I was told that she would take my pulses. Unlike traditional “medical pulses” there were 12 in this form of acupuncture. From these she could tell which of the five elements were out of balance. With her needles she could then begin to restore that balance, she could begin the healing process.

I listened intently to her explanation. It resonated with every cell of my body. That is until she said these words which sent me hiding behind my wall of insecurity “We have to talk for about an hour before I place the needles so I can understand what is going on with you.”

Immediately I began to sink into the chair. I could not make myself small enough. If I could have dug a hole and crawled in it I would have. The fear of speaking to her, for an hour no less, was beyond my imagination, beyond my capability at that time. I was now in panic mode.

All I could do was point to my ankle and say in a voice that quaked “No. Just the ankle. Traditional will be fine.”

And so it went for two more sessions. “How’s the ankle?” Shawna would ask.

“Better” was my only response.

“Ready for 5 Element yet?”

“No. Just the ankle today.”

On the fourth visit every thing changed. The time for 5 Element had arrived. The beauty of Shawna’s Healing and her magic needles would change my life forever that day, and every day since then. Together they would save my live.

Chapter 22

The Dark Cloud

I was anxious, nervous to see Shawna that day. I felt as though I were in some deep dark abyss with no way out. It felt as if there was a dark cloud hanging over my head. There was no joy, only sadness and despair. The escape route from this abyss eluded me. Deep in my Heart, I knew; with a capital K, that Shawna and her 5 Elements could help me. For the first time in my life I was beginning to trust someone.

It was with a walk of depression that I entered the Sanctuary of my little closet that day. Head down, shoulders slumped forward, with shuffled steps I took my place on the chair in the corner. Shawna intuitively knew something was wrong. She placed her hand on my shoulder. I could feel only love flowing through my body from her hand.

"What's wrong?" she said. "Is it time for 5 Element?" I shook my head "Yes."

"What are you feeling?"

My mind began to spin. Feelings. A place I didn't like to go. For so long I stuffed them down, down into a place where I thought they would never surface. I was suppose to be the strong one of my family. Yet in reality I was not. I kept such a tight rein on my feelings that they were never allowed to run free.

I had made that vow when I was about 9 years old. Now, after many sessions with the Puzzle Master it seems quite silly; but it was all my 9 year old mind knew to do. During that year I had had tonsillitis almost every month. No sooner would it clear and it would be back. So as was the custom in those days, my tonsils were removed. No longer constantly ill, no longer running fevers of 102 almost every day, my metabolism slowed down. In one year I gained 20 pounds.

At the start of the new school year, my mother took us to buy new school clothes. Needless to say after gaining 20 pounds, none of my clothes fit. I must have tried on 15 dresses in the dressing room that day, and not a single one fit, no matter the size. My mother said "You are so fat, nothing fits you. I should just send you to school naked."

I began to cry. Even at 9 I was so embarrassed, so humiliated that even my mother was calling me fat. The saleslady must have heard me crying and came in "Is anything the matter?" she asked.

My mother said, "No. Everything is okay. She is just hot and sweaty that's all."

At that moment I vowed that no one, no one would every make me cry again. That never would I be humiliated like that again. That I would rather die than let anyone know how I felt. It was the best solution my 9 year old could come up with. It was still the solution I was using at 50.

These are the thoughts that were racing through my mind at the posing of Shawna's question. It would be many months before she read this story.

I heard her ask again "What are you feeling?"

All I could say was "There is a dark cloud over my head." Nothing more.

I was only Shawna's second 5 Element patient; "Little Mary" being the first. She used every skill she had, every trick that she knew to get me to speak to her in more than one or two word sentences. I know that my answers of "Yes. No. Good" were frustrating to her. After all, talking was a major part of the 5 Element treatment. Later she would tell others of this first meeting, describing how it was like "pulling hens teeth."

Out of this frustration came the answer for both of us. She said to me four words; words that opened a whole new world that began the healing. Those four words were "Write me a story."

Chapter 23

Write Me a Story

With the saying of those four words, “Write me a story,” I felt freedom. I felt that this was a way to finally release the reins, if even just a little. It was as if a giant weight had been lifted off my shoulders. That which has been hidden for so long now has a way out.

“I will gladly write you a story” I told her.

Shawna said “Great. Write me a story about your perfect world. What are your hopes and dream? What are your goals? Tell me what your perfect world would look like.”

The next week I walked in with story in hand. We took our designated places, Shawna on the table, me in the chair. She asked “How was your treatment last week?”

“Good” I replied.

“Did you do your homework?”

I did not speak. I merely handed her my story. I could not watch as she first began to read my words which now had a voice, "What if she doesn't like it?" I thought.

After awhile I couldn't help but glance up every so often to see the reaction in her eyes. I was surprised to see that on occasion they seemed misty. I waited silently while she finished reading this, my story.

May 2003

In My Perfect World

i would have ocean front mountain property with a log cabin so i could wake and sleep to the gentle pulse of Mother Earth as the waves breathe in and out against the shore. There would be an "ocean" pool in which to swim so that i could partake of the ocean's energy, realign my internal "pulse" with hers when needed and glean the wisdom from all the creatures who reside there. There would be a humpback whale or two who would visit often and would allow me to enjoy their play, their songs, and their antics as they jump and breech, free in the ocean. And since it would be a "perfect world" they would allow me to touch them and see deep into their eyes and share their wisdom with me.

There would be pine trees; providing the sweet smell of pine to freshen the air as it mixes with the salty mist of the ocean. Pines to provide shade from the heat with large trunks to hug to keep me grounded. Limbs that sway in the breeze to the rhythm of the waves below. There would be a garden to plant flowers.

There would be a significant other who was kind, gentle, non-abusive, nurturing and loving who would hold and cuddle me and visa versa. Someone with a sense of humor who would laugh at my corny jokes and who could make me laugh as well. Someone who will be a partner on the path of growth spiritually, mentally and emotionally. Serious when needed yet able to play.

Included would be a circle of "friends." a select few who come to play, enjoy the arts, sit in silence and enjoy each others presence. Friends to have lively conversations, to discuss philosophy or spirituality. The kind who can "walk in the rain" and not just get wet. Friends who can just be silly when the need arises.

i would have my cats and perhaps a dog. Nothing like a cold wet nose for an alarm clock; or a purring ball of fluff to warm your lap.

As for me...i would be more in balance; enough work to keep me stimulated, enough play to keep me young. i would have the energy to work, play, exercise; calmness to sleep. i would spend less time in "grizzly bear." i would not let my past influence my present or my future. i would not be ruled by my fear. i would have enough self confidence and self esteem to remove my armor and let the marshmallow inside out. I would always be learning and growing. i would have time to read just for the pleasure, time for photography, time to write. i would have the health to play sports again and hike in the mountains.

There would be conversations to stimulate my mind, mud puddles to jump in, an ocean to calm me, friends and animals for company and loving arms to hold me...all in a place called "MY PERFECT WORLD."

When she finished reading I thought I saw a tear in her

eye reflected by the candle light. Thinking I had done something wrong to elisite those tears I asked if this was so?

"No" she replied. "This is beautiful."

I didn't know what to say, so I said nothing. It was beyond my imagination to think that someone would find my words beautiful, but she did. And because she did the words flowed, healing occurred, lessons were learned; all from four little words, "write me a story."

Chapter 24

The Puzzle Master Appears

This was indeed a time of darkness. No part of my life seemed to be in balance, not work or play or sleep. The NICU (Neonatal Intensive Care Unit) where I worked was beyond crazy. There were upwards of 45 infants to care for and one was more ill than the next. Many nights I had neither time to eat or drink. The only time I sat down was to write orders. By the time I got home I was exhausted but could not sleep. I ran the night through my mind trying to figure out what I could do better. And play; there was no time or energy.

If I was not thinking about work, I was lying in bed trying to figure out the purpose, the cause of this darkness. It seemed the more I thought about it, the more energy I fed it, the worse it got. The darkness even affected my self esteem, which was not in the best of places before. I felt I had no significance. Thus when I wrote I used the little i.

There are no accidents, no coincidences. A picture on the wall that I had looked at a hundred times, but never really "seen" provided the initial catalyst. With the guidance of Shawna and her magic needles as I call them, a true "Aha" moment occurred.

June 9, 2003

The Puzzle Master

There is a Chinese character hanging from my wall which has alluded my attention these many days and months. Yesterday it stirred upon the wall as if to say "Look, look here!" i approached this framed character with the intent but to straighten it upon the wall. As i reached to place it in alignment it seemed to tilt at just the right angle so that i could read the message it contained. The character was "CHAOS" and below it stated "Brings order out of confusion."

On the shelf next to this image just happened to be a copy of the I Ching. i opened it and turned to "chaos." there it spoke of times of growth being beset with difficulties, that in these times of new beginnings everything is still unformed and dark. How one needs helpers to overcome the chaos.

At last…a name for this feeling i have been having, "chaos." It has indeed been a time of darkness where nothing seemed to have order or balance. The pieces of the puzzle were so far apart that it was almost impossible to imagine that they had a relationship at all. i had to travel so far from one piece to the next that i forgot what the first piece revealed and was unable to find its mate. The puzzle remained without form and seemingly with out purpose.

Then an injury; the spraining of an ankle which seemed then not to heal. Was this perhaps the Universe saying "You have wished to no longer run from this chaos. You wish to place form to the unformed, you wish the darkness to be absorbed into the light. Let us together form this 'injury' so that you can not run and perhaps find your answers."

Amongst old papers about to be thrown out; a single page falls gently to the floor. i reach down and discover a brochure about acupuncture. About to throw it out, instead i place it on the counter where it resides for another two weeks. Now in even more pain and darkness i finally call and make an appointment; truly thinking it was for my ankle alone.

Yet now i realize that i was being lead to find a "Healer" who would help in this process of chaos; of a new growth. How is it that i arrived with a sprained ankle hoping for relief, and discovered a "Puzzle Master" hidden in this sacred space. Slowly she helps me begin to find the pieces of the puzzle. Some are scattered close, some afar; others are farther away still…from yet another life, another time and space. Some are still hidden, waiting patiently to be discovered.

This Puzzle Master started with but a single piece, a sprained ankle. The only piece i could recognize in the darkness and the chaos. She showed it to me many times and it remained the same. Then one day as the Puzzle Master was again showing me this piece, a tiny quirk of light emerged from the darkness. That tiniest bit of illumination was just enough to see a pattern emerge onto the piece. It transformed before my eyes as the faintest glow of a heart was revealed.

"'Tis magic" i thought. How is it that an ankle could become a heart? As her lessons continued, more quirks of light gathered, now forming atoms of light. Enough to illuminate the most important, pivotal piece so it could be seen clearly. "Look closely" she said. "Look with your spiritual eyes. Listen to it speak with your spiritual ears." Being the dutiful student i did as i was told.

i began to examine the piece, first only seeing the ankle, nothing more. But then i began to "see" the piece not merely "look." i examined it for many moments or perhaps only a millisecond in Universal time. i discovered that hidden in this one piece was the entire puzzle. The pattern of the whole contained in each single piece.

Together we took those pieces and placed them together, their stems and holes interlocking tightly. Energy was flowing between them as they communicated back and forth with one another. And i "saw" that although each piece was separate; each piece also contained the whole and was connected to the whole. Yet the whole also defined the separate pieces. Form from the formless, light from the darkness…perhaps now growth.

How very lucky that i found this Puzzle Master disguised as a Healer, or perhaps it is a Healer disguised as a Puzzle Master. Or perhaps they are just different aspects of the same being. And to think i almost threw away her calling card.

i am thankful for the chaos and the sprained ankle for without them i would not have found the Puzzle Master or the opportunity to grow.

A seed must first endure the darkness of the earth before it can burst forth into the light and grow.

I have reread this story many times. Although it was one of the first, it started my growth process, my healing. Growth can not occur in a static state. One must have action, movement in order to grow and heal. Standing still only keeps you in the "same place."

A single step is all it takes and the journey will begin. It matters not if it is interpreted as a "right" or "wrong" direction, for which ever way you go is correct. Adjustment can be made along the way. One can not adjust stillness, for by definition it is "non-movement."

I also learned that one does need a "helper." In my case it has been Shawna; whom I am honored to call my best Friend; and the part of her which is Healer and Puzzle Master. And of course her magic needles and 5 Element Acupuncture. I have found that "toughing it out alone" is not the answer. It only keeps you in the self imposed prison of darkness.

Chapter 25

The Bud

As time went on I did begin to speak more. I trusted Shawna and the Puzzle Master more each week, and with that trust my voice began to emerge; slowly ever so slowly. Yet my stories were still our prime means of communication.

Each week something miraculous would always occur in our sessions. It still does after all these years. The "sacred closet" was that and more. It was becoming my "portal" to universes and dimensions I never imagined existed.

Shawna, with her extraordinary gifts and talents as Healer, her connection to the Universe and God, her magic needles could send me on journeys far beyond the bounds of planet earth. It was here that I began to learn my lessons.

Since the age of 9 I had protected my self from harm; I

thought; by wrapping my self in armor, by closing my bud. In my 9 year old wisdom I thought it would repel all harmful arrows which came my way. Little did I know that as well as keeping things from getting in, it also prevented anything from getting out. This day I would be shown a different perspective.

June 2003

The Bud

In a small room, no more than 5 by 7 feet, the Puzzle Master has created a Sacred Space. A space where sacred lessons are taught both small and large, where gifts from the Universe seem abundant and great transformations occur. i seem once again to be a humble recipient of these most precious gifts.

i am never sure what lesson will emerge from this space and the time spent there; for it seems to be a port, a channel to the Universe and Its Knowledge. i come each week with open Mind and Heart, with my "ears which do not hear" and my "eyes which do not see" and patiently await for the lesson to unfold.

And so the lesson began this day; the Puzzle Master imparting her knowledge, i listening and attempting to synthesize and embody the knowledge. Once again my ear began to burn; the sensation i have now come to know as energy; a cue to listen with my special ears. As i tuned in words escaped from my mouth. i heard only "...pain of the bud...blossom." Then silently the message continued "The day is near, meditate upon these words." "Wait" i thought, "i have missed some of the words. Try again!"

There was only silence. Far in the distance i could

hear the Puzzle Master say something about "very profound" and "where did that come from" as i was pulled quickly back to the present time and space. What words is she speaking of i thought. What ever they were i am NOT the originator of them. i don't know where they came from. Perhaps it was something i read or saw somewhere. But then again perhaps i was momentarily in that port or channel of Universal Knowledge, for it was strange that the Puzzle Master's words seemed so distant and far away when i know she was no more than two feet away.

The lesson continued, now with the needles which seemed to have such a profound effect on me. i remember the Puzzle Master saying something about "rebirth" as i drifted into a meditative state; a golden needle divining the faintest glow of golden white light around me as i left.

A "bud" appeared in my mind's eye. Is this the bud spoken of earlier i thought? i need to know the missing words! The androgynous voice began to speak again, "The day will come when the pain of remaining a bud will be more than the pain of blossoming." There was a resonance of my entire Being with these words as i began to contemplate their meaning.

i began to see a vision sometime early in my existence as the bud attempting to bloom. It's bloom was deemed unworthy. It's beauty denied. It was some how unfit to exist. And the bud gathered the few petals which had attempted to bloom around itself very tightly. It was an attempt to protect its Heart, its Soul, its very Existence, which lay at the core of its being.

i watched as if an observer now, as the life of the bud progressed. It continued to bind its pedals close. On an occasion as rare as the Blue Moon, an attempt would be made to once again allow the bud to bloom. But the result always seemed the same, in the end the bloom was not worthy. So the bud gathered its pedals more tightly than ever, adding a layer of armor for further protection. And it began to believe in its own unworthiness. Pain radiated deep from within the core. It was now painful to be the bud. Yet it seemed contending with the KNOWN pain of the bud outweighed the UNKNOWN pain of the bloom.

From this observers vantage point i began to see how the tightly held pedals and the coat of armor were now strangling the very things they were designed to protect. The Heart unable to function while bound in the core; it could not pump its life-giving fluid. Nor could it love or be loved in this bound state. The very Soul of the bud seemed to be fading away.

The Essence of the bud somehow seemed to have survived, coiled tightly within a cocoon at the core. Weak, tired from the fight, but alive none the less. A tiny crack appeared in the cocoon, allowing an atom of the Essence to escape. It turned and twisted as it maneuvered its way through the tightly bound pedals trying to reach the summit. With its last micron of energy, it pushed a pedal back just enough to emerge into the Light. There it rested.

The Light began to renew its energy. It became stronger. And with the strength came a voice; softer than a whisper, perceptible only with "ears which do not hear." The Essence began to communicate with the bud. "There is nothing to fear here. There is only Love and Light and the endless possibilities of things to come. Inside there is only darkness, loneliness, pain and the Untruth of worthlessness. With all MY BEING I tell you, it is worth the risk." And i watched as my Soul wept.

And so i believe that today may be the day that the pain of remaining the bud outweighs the pain of blossoming. i am not sure that the bud will bloom fully in this lifetime. There are so many pedals and it seems so little time is left. i am ready to take the risk; to attempt "rebirth of the blossom." i may require some assistance though as these pedals and armor have been bound to the bud for so long. i can not guarantee that a pedal or 2 or 3 or 10 may not recoil back to the core, but i can promise to take "the risk." For i can think of no safer place to bloom than in this most Sacred 5 by 7 room. A place of transformation; the Puzzle Master at my side as my guide. My intuition tells me she is as grand a Master at "gardening" as she is at puzzles.

It was one of the hardest tasks I have <u>ever</u> undertaken in my life; to unfold the bud. The process continues to this day; for there are pedals which resist opening; still clinging to the untruth.

Yet it has been the most rewarding adventure I have ever undertaken. I found that I was killing that which I was trying to save, my very Essence. And that that which kept it bound was untrue, was a lie.

Where once I was afraid of hugs, to unworthy you see; I now have an abundance of them in my life. I would not trade even one of them for all the monies in the Universe. Now instead of recoiling in fear, my Heart sings with joy, for it deserves Love.

The suit of armor which was constructed of "unworthiness" only acted as a magnate to attract those which confirmed this lie. Many supposed “friends” had told me that I was “not good enough” for them and disappeared from my life. A boyfriend or two had the same opinion.

But as my bud began to open, these people seemed to drop from my life. The Universal law of “like attracts like” was in play here.

Now I have people in my life like Shawna and a Universal Family who love me for who I truly am; not the lies of the past.

The TRUTH will set you free!

Chapter 26

The Rose and the Vase

I am not sure that anything "normal" ever occurred in our Sacred Space. Then again perhaps what occurs there is normal and it is "the real world" which is the illusion.

There was however a pattern which each session followed. Shawna and I would talk; usually briefly for I was still finding my voice and the courage to use it. She would then read my story for the week; the lesson that I learned; the Wisdom that I gleaned from her and the Puzzle Master. More times than not this included tears, not from me but Shawna. It still amazes me that my combination of letters into words can elicit such emotion in another.

Then I would lay upon the table; a table that would become my portal to Universal Wisdom. Here my pulses would be taken, all 12 of them. The combination of my story and what my pulses "said" would guide Shawna on the placement of the magic healing needles. Yet as time went on; and Shawna's connection to the Universe became stronger; she would be able to receive point locations without ever touching my pulses. It has been my privilege and honor to watch this growth and be the recipient of its gifts.

With the placement of each needle I would get closer to the portal. It was taking less and less time for me to actually pass through its doors. My journeys were exceeding the bounds of this earth plane; and they were becoming more intense, more vivid. This journey was no exception. It was actually a lesson for us both. It came in the form of flowers.

August 2003

This was a most unique session. i can say i have never received flowers like that before. Sometimes i "see" pictures; little snapshots of things which seem to have relevance; pieces of lessons or guidance i suppose. As an example my friend Sue in California was wondering about us and the relationship with a man she knew. Suddenly there was a picture of us as Druids in the forest. It continued with other pictures as if looking through a photo album. Each picture came with a caption or commentary to explain it.

This is what happened the other day in that most special healing room; portal to magical places. i will try my best to recreate it for you as the lesson seemed to be for both of us.

i am not sure exactly what you saw, but i saw a very large vase; a Ming vase. Inside this vase was it seemed 100 roses or more in varying stages of bud and blossom. i can not remember ever smelling roses so sweet as these. After you left the roses and the vase seemed to just float before me. i did not see anyone but it was as if there was a presence who gently placed their hands upon my shoulders as if in an act of reassurance as the commentary began. It was one of the few times i have actually stayed in my body during a treatment. i believe that same presence is here now to help me recreate the message.

"It is because you see in pictures that we have given you this gift of the roses and the vase. A gift to you both, a lesson hidden within. It is a continuation of that which was written to the Puzzle Master."

"You are both as the vase and the rose. One more rose, the other more vase, yet each possesses qualities of the other. The vase separate is but a container. The rose separate is but a flower. The vase illuminates the qualities of the rose and the rose in return illuminates the qualities of the vase. Together they are more than the other alone. (The picture here was one of the vase alone, the roses to the side. Indeed it was not as spectacular as the combination. They then recombined into a spectacular display).

"The roses represent aspects of yourself and others who come to the Healer. Each rose or aspect in different stages of bloom. Neither the rose or the Healer should be discouraged by that which does not bloom; for some will remain buds by choice while others will require more time to blossom. It is the combination of both bud and bloom which creates interest and adventure within the arrangement."

It is impossible to describe in words the feelings which went with this "vision" and so i will not even attempt to try.

But i think that i understand its meaning. We are both teacher and student. Sometimes one more than the other. There is no teacher without a student and there is no student without a teacher. The student becomes better because of the teacher and the teacher is better because of the student. Each progresses faster than they would have alone.

The second part i believe has a duel meaning. For the first part i myself was struggling with the thoughts that now that the "blooming" process has begun i want all the flowers to bloom, NOW. Yet there seems to be those that are resistant; some that are partially open and some that are in full bloom. i understand now that some may take more time than the others while some may never open. That they can not bloom all at once.

And so it goes for the lessons i am to learn this lifetime. Some i will learn completely, some partially, some not at all. This is what will give interest and adventure to this lifetime.

The other message i believe is for the nurturer, the Healer, the Teacher in all of us. There will be individuals that are encountered in varying stages of blossom to bud. There will be those who will be helped and there are those that will not be able to be "fixed" for they are not yet ready to be "cured" or ready for the lesson. And that is okay. It is sometimes from these individuals that we learn the most; usually about ourselves. They are our greatest teachers.

This i believe is the message of the vase and the rose. In some ways it is hard to recreate it exactly. The "feeling" part i can not translate as of yet. i have done my best with the words and symbols i have available.

Thanks to the Universe and the Puzzle Master for this wonderful gift!

Chapter 27

Armor

Over the last few weeks I had been struggling with seeing the glass half full instead of half empty. I was trying to see that the reality I had created was the illusion not the other way around. The illusion was trying to changing into a butterfly. Yet I was resisting; for the cocoon felt so tight around my body I could hardly breathe.

She told me of a "Husband and Wife" split. "It is when we lose touch with our true nature," she said. "The result is the creation of a false self based on our erroneous interpretations of life experiences." It was amazing to watch Shawna transform into the Puzzle Master, Teacher and Mentor as she spoke these words. I was so caught up in the transformation, I almost missed the message. But the talents and gifts of the Puzzle Master and her 5 Element needles; along with my journey brought the message home.

<u>August 2003</u>

You spoke of a "Husband and Wife" split as you felt my pulses this day. i believe you said something about struggle between two opposites, at least that is what i heard. Perhaps because that is where i am at present; changing the perspective from half empty to half full. Seeing that the death of the caterpillar not as a tragedy but as a wonderful beginning as a butterfly. It is this journey, this transformation that i have begun. Yet often when i peer into my backpack of things i have with me on this journey i find things of the caterpillar which do not serve the butterfly. Sometimes it is difficult to give up those familiar things in order to make room for butterfly wings.

Today another step in the transformation, in the blooming. As i lay on the table i could feel the armor. It felt almost as a tortoise shell held on with bands of steel. The bands loose, not as tight as in previous days. i began to feel hands upon my back running down to the base of my spine. The hands moved to the base of the "shell" and began to gently pry it loose. Little by little the shell began to loosen. Occasionally a scalpel was used to cut through some of the most stubborn adhesions. At the same time other loving hands were loosening the steel bands around my chest, put there as reinforcements to insure adherence of the armor. As they loosened there was a feeling of ah; at last the ability to take a full deep breath. The armor now about half removed. Salve applied to the new raw skin, having not been exposed for many years. As the hands left there was assurance that they would be back to complete the mission. Time was needed to adjust, to recover they said. With the opening of the door they bid goodbye, returning to the realm from which they came.

Now with the loosening of the bands and the armor, somehow it feels like there is more room, more room inside to both give and receive. More room for life itself. Slowly i am beginning to understand this concept of giving and receiving, Of how in order to continue to give one must receive. It is kind of like a bank account. You can not continue to make withdrawals if nothing is being placed into the account. Eventually the account runs dry; even if it is interest bearing. i understand that receiving makes the giving better. That in order to receive one must make room by giving and in order to give one must make room for receiving. i have the concept, now i just need to continue to put it into practice.

Perhaps of all that i have received most recently, hugs and a new "Friend" have been the most important. i did not realize the impact of hugs. From my previous perspective i was more worried about "doing it right." Did i hug too hard, too easy? Do i put my arms on the top or on the bottom and so on? There was not much hugging in my house growing up, at least that i remember. It is hard to do something if you don't practice. Even more so what if i give it and it is rejected? Better to not try than do it wrong or experience rejection yet again.

Yet over these last few weeks and months things have changed. As the bud has begun to bloom and the armor has begun to lift, there seems to be more room inside. More room to store that which is given and that which is received. Now i know that i can't really "do it wrong." And with that knowledge I can now hug with total joy and abandonment. i am beginning to actually enjoy hugs, both giving and receiving.

As each new transformation day continues i am glad that not all my wishes have been granted. For if they had i would not be here today. i would not have had the joy of finding an old and trusted "friend." Between junior high and high school i prayed to the Universe every night that i would die, that i would not wake up in the morning. And every morning much to my dismay i woke up; only looking forward to the next night in hopes that my prayer would be answered then. After awhile i stopped praying; thinking the Universe did not hear me, did not care either. Now, today i know better. i am so thankful that wish was not granted. i would be missing out on the best part of my life so far.

It seems like only yesterday and yet so long ago those same feelings began to bubble up again. And what to my wondering eyes should appear but the Puzzle Master. Through a series of events only the Universe could have orchestrated, and with the help of the Puzzle Master, a transformation has begun to occur. Now i wake up each day eager to see what will happen next; what adventure, what lesson i will learn. Do you not see…you have saved my life!

i can never see you as "just the person who places the needles." Can you understand? You are a "Light worker," a "way Shower," and as you said a "Wounded Healer." Yet in some ways it is your woundedness which allows you to be such a wonderful Healer and Way Shower. You are the Way Shower because you have been down the same path of hurt and pain. You have the experience to say "I was there and now I am here. You can do it too. Follow the path." And yet if it were possible i would take away your pain.

Most of all i treasure your friendship. i am so thankful that you chose to incarnate this lifetime. As it says in *Illusions*: "Meeting again after moments or lifetimes, is certain for those who are friends." i will not ever take it for granted, for it has been such a long journey to find it and you again. i am honored and humbled to have you as "Friend" and be called *"Friend"* in return. i give to you companionship along the path, encouragement and joy in your growth even if it means you grow beyond me. i share your pain, multiply your joy. If i could give you one thing, i would give you the ability to see yourself through my eyes and all the others which you have helped…then you would realize what a truly special person you are! Thank you for being in my world. You encourage me to go beyond myself. What a wonderful gift you have given me!

It is a strange place that we have all come to learn our life lessons; this planet called Earth. For it seems that reality is illusion and illusion is the true reality. i believed that the tightly closed bud surrounded in armor to protect it was truly reality. Now i am beginning to see that that was the illusion. The bud in full bloom surrounded by love, returning that love; once thought to be only a dream is now becoming reality. The most amazing part is that i can begin to see that this has always been the reality. It has been a very long and often times painful journey thus far. i know the journey has just begun and there are "miles to go before i sleep." Now i have companions with me on this difficult and joyous road; Trust, Faith, and most important of all a "Friend."

Shawna and I would have to "agree to disagree" on her role in my healing over the years. She contended she was "Just the person who placed the needles." I of course would disagree.

If not for her connection to the Universe and God, if not for her intuitiveness, if not for her ability to Know the exact points to send me on these healing journeys, if not for her gifts and talents as Healer which she so gladly shares, I would not be where I am today. For I am a blossom without armor, a caterpillar who flies. How sweet is that?

Always, always will she be more than "just the person who places needles." This book of journeys I offer as my evidence to that truth. For what she does for one, she does for all.

Chapter 28

Fear

For the first time in a long time I was allowing emotion to bubble up inside me. I still did not have the courage to let them out, but I was at least beginning to acknowledge them. The emotion which predominated was none other than fear.

Shawna and I along with her mom were preparing to go to a conference in Boston. It was a conference on how to develop your intuitiveness. Yet all I was developing was fear.

The three of us were to spend 5 days together. Although Shawna and I were becoming friends, we still had not spent that much time together. I knew more the Puzzle Master than Shawna the person. And I had never met her mom. Now we were not only going to spend 5 nights in a hotel, but we were going to spend 8 hours in a plane together.

My bud may have started to bloom, but I was still scared to death. Unknown to me; the Puzzle Master and the Universe had a journey planned for me.

September 2003

This was one of the more emotional sessions that i have had thus far. Perhaps it has something to do with listening to the tapes. After all it does say that one will become more sensitive…maybe that means it is working. Perhaps it is from the further opening of the bud. Perhaps it is occurring the closer the death of the caterpillar and the birth of the butterfly arrives. These emotions are bubbling to the surface slowly but surely.

Now for the journey; a most powerful one. As you were running your most intuitive fingers along my ankle you felt anger. i could feel it as well; tender under your fingers almost screaming for attention. Yet at first i did not know from where this anger came. "Go to the water" you said and as always the dutiful student that is where i went. To the ocean, home, safety. Here i began walking along the beach; splashing in the surf. Feeling the energy, the comfort of the water. As i splashed in the surf i looked up and saw a cave hidden amongst the cliffs. There was enough light to illuminate the entrance and slightly beyond. The sandy floor inviting; the walls a shelter from the wind. Perhaps an adventure waiting for me inside. And so i entered the archway of the cave.

The cave became darker as i forged ahead. As the last bit of light was about to fade a torch appeared on the sandy floor. i picked it up and lit it; now my flashlight in the darkness. As i proceeded farther into the cave i came to a large open area. In the middle was a chair of sorts; a boulder with the middle worn as if a seat. On the wall opposite the chair, a place for the torch to be hung. i placed the torch in its holder and the room was illuminated just enough to vanquish the darkness. i sat in the chair and stared at the carving and paintings from long ago which graced the cave walls. A natural spring bubbled off to the side. Perhaps a sacred place i thought.

As i sat in my boulder chair i heard a voice, neither male nor female begin to speak, "You have come here because you seek answers. It is here you may find them; if you are willing to look."

i closed my eyes and slowly drifted away with the voice. i need to know where this anger is coming from. i can not dissipate it until i know what it is about. I sat there for what seemed hours but am sure it was only seconds in the time-space of the cave. Slowly, as the fountain before me, the feeling of fear began to bubble up. That is it i thought. i am angry at this fear which has taken over my life. Even more so i am angry at myself for giving it my power. How could i be so stupid? How could I have given away my power to this fear?

i do not even know when it began to take over. Somewhere in childhood; perhaps it has been there for lifetimes. It projects many fingers into my life, this fear. There is fear of not doing it right no matter what IT is giving birth to perfectionism; a goal i seldom reach leading only to frustration. Fear of abandonment; of giving my heart, my soul, my "Heart-space" love to another and then having it not returned or later rejected. Thrown to the wayside as they continue down the road. Fear of removing the armor completely, of exposing the sensitive marshmallow inside, of opening the flood gates of tears which reside there and may never stop once started.

i am tired of this fear. i am tired of letting it run my life. i am tired of the struggle. And so i shout into the darkness "Tell me. How do i overcome this fear? How do i stop this struggle which is about to drowned me?"

The voice which had spoken earlier returned. It replied "Stop struggling. It is that simple. As long as you lend your energy to struggling and fear that is what you will get; more fear and more to struggle against. Do not concentrate on the fear of losing but on the joy of giving and receiving, even if it is only for a second in space-time. Do not morn the loss of the rock shell but rejoice in the release of the marshmallow insides which have yearned to be free for so long. It is the difference between seeing the glass half full and half empty. Simple yes. Easy perhaps. That is up to you; for you and you alone will dictate the ease with which you make the transition. It does not mean however that you must do it alone." The voice faded back into the recesses of the cave from which it originated. i was left alone to contemplate this new yet familiar knowledge.

i began to imagine what it might feel like to give and receive love without the fear of it being taken away. To be totally engulfed in the joy of NOW instead of caught in the fear of the past or future. To have the armor removed. The pressure behind the flood gates released as the marshmallow insides flow freely, able to express. i imagined doing, just doing without the pressure of perfection. It was a wonderful and joyous feeling. My heart, my Soul happy as well.

As the Puzzle Master was calling me home, the voice returned one last time. "If you can feel it, if you can imagine it, if you can see it, you can do it." The door to the portal opened and as i stepped through the cave vanished.

I took this lesson with me to Boston. I concentrated on the glass being full instead of half empty. I vowed that I would not give my power to fear. I will not lie; at times it was a struggle but each day it got easier and easier. I actually talked to them both for hours at the end of each night; and I didn't die.

At the end of those five days I found that I had been given numerous Blessings. I begin to retake my power back from fear.

Best of all; I now had 2 friends, actual "Friends" in my life. They are still my Friends to this day, part of my Universal family. A family of Love and understanding.

Chapter 29

Confrontation

Not my best subject I tell my self and so it is true. Just the thought of it makes me quake in my boots. I would avoid it, as one would avoid the plague.

I always associated conflict and confrontation with "loud screaming voices." That is what I remember from my childhood. I never learned to resolve a conflict, to stand up for myself or my beliefs. The lesson I learned was that if one "gave in," kept quite and did what one was asked, the screaming would stop; eventually.

Yelling back was not an option for me for as the Puzzle Master could tell you. "Loud" was not how one would describe my voice. I had the voice which corresponded to my element; metal, for it was soft and had the sound of weeping. Often times the Puzzle Master would tell me just the opposite of what a parent would usually say to a child.

She would tell me "Use your 'outside' voice. I can barely hear you." My outside voice was no better, for it was just above a whisper.

The Universe had a new lesson planned. It was as much about growth as it was about confrontation. The metamorphosis of the caterpillar was continuing; coming ever closer to the emergence of the butterfly from the cocoon. It was time for me to see how close it really was.

I was still attending classes with Mary Beth (from here on MBO) the preacher. We had moved the "church" to her home since there were now only 7 students left in our little congregation. MBO referred to us as the "Sacred Seven," the ones who would be with her for life.

Yet with each passing day I felt more and more uncomfortable in these classes. I would talk in our Master Mind groups of how Shawna and her 5 Element Acupuncture were helping me so much, helping me to grow. Yet MBO would tell us how things like psychiatry and acupuncture were "not the answer," were not helpful. How she had the answer if we were only smart enough to hear it, to understand it.

I told the Puzzle Master of my dilemma, of my conflict. I did not want to stay, yet I was too afraid to leave. I felt as if I were caught between a rock and a hard place.

With all the Wisdom of a Sage and that of Puzzle Master she said, "It is time. It is time for you to see your growth. Time for your little wood sapling to make it's appearance. You can do this. You are strong enough. We can do this together." Yet I fought for my "weakness" not my strength.

Dearest Friend and Puzzle Master;

i think you might know what i am about to say, yes

it is about class. After much thought, contemplation and internal struggle, "i don't want to go back!" i don't want to stay yet the thought of leaving terrifies me! It is that same feeling of trying to leave an abusive relationship or dare i say cult; caught between a rock and a hard place. i can't stay yet do not know how to get out. Death would be the only acceptable reason to MBO to leave. And i am sorry to say that for a brief moment it was on my list of options. If only i could run away. But i know that would not solve anything.

You see there is so much conflict involved. My internal struggle to leave, the absolute terror i feel just thinking about confronting her, and my desire to not "hurt" her in the process. For you see MBO thinks that i am one of the "Sacred Seven" as she puts it; bound to be with her for life. Telling her i was leaving would certainly be hitting her blind sided as she has no idea that i would ever think of leaving. It seems not a nice thing to do to somebody. Yet i can hear her telling me how disappointed in me she is for me leaving. That sort of "how dare you, pretending to be on of the devoted few." How now there will be financial concerns because i do give a lot of money to the Center (one must tithe you know). This is but one of many scenarios i have created in my mind. Others are much worse, only one better.

Would she truly practice what she preaches and be non-judgmental and then detach from the situation? Would she truly let me speak my truth without telling me how wrong i am? Will i be seen and branded a Judas? Would i be hearing how could i do this to her and leave the Center in such financial straights? i do not know the answer. How will i be able to speak my truth to her? i think there is not enough "wood" in all the Universe to back me up.

And so here i sit between a rock and a hard place. Unable to breathe as i think about it; feeling as though i have been punched in the stomach and all air has escaped my lungs. My heart beating 200 times a minute, my hands shaking. Terror and anxiety filling my body. All self confidence gone. Please show me the way.

The Puzzle Master worked on my water (fear) and wood (strength, self esteem) for two sessions. We talked of the Universal Law of "where the mind goes the energy flows." Imagine the best scenario for the best outcome. Do not listen to the old tapes for they are illusion, ego. "You CAN do this" was repeated over and over by the Puzzle Master. My hope was that those words would replace the old tape of "No you can't." She had more Faith in me than I had in myself.

Yet as with my bud; it was becoming more painful, more distressing to stay than to leave. Staying was not for my highest good; that I knew. Armed with the courage of my Eagle, my little oak sapling, and the support of the Puzzle Master I confronted MBO.

November 2003

Dearest Friend, Puzzle Master and now Singer of Songs;

You are indeed a miracle worker! i have not the words to express how truly grateful i am for all you have done. i could not have done it without you, your incredible tools and talents, and your tremendous support. i thank you with my whole Being.

When last you saw me i was in an abyss. As abyss so deep i knew not how to escape. i seemed to have forgotten all that i knew. My knowledge left at the surface when i fell into the deep dark hole. i could find no tools to escape; not even a screwdriver was to be had.

Enter the Puzzle Master; a quirk of Light in the black hole of darkness. Enough Light to be able to say the darkness is not total darkness now. With that quirk came the ability to escape. It was almost as if i could hear the Puzzle Master's voice in my head saying "If you can put film on a canister in total darkness you can find the tools to escape the abyss. We can do this together. Stop a moment and look for them with your eyes which do not see for it is they that see in the darkness when human eyes can not. Look for the window."

With that "thought" in my mind i headed for the table and the Puzzle Master began her work. "Go to the top of the trees" she says. "A large window, easy to walk through, will be waiting." Needles beginning to be placed, the journey begins.

i find myself transported to the same dark room as my previous encounter with the "window." Only this time i do not have to wait for the window to form in the dark walls. As i feel myself materializing in the room; there, already waiting for me is a window the size of the entire wall. The same emerald green silk curtains adorn its boarders. A gentle breeze blows through the open panes. Without hesitation i run through the opening, arms spread, Knowing that the Eagle in me would be on the other side.

Indeed, as i fall from the window, chocolate brown feathers appear on my wings. Catching an updraft i soar above the now familiar tree tops. Golden white light warms me as i glide upon the air currents. Transmuted into Eagle, i do so enjoy this feeling of freedom that flight gives me. And so i fly a little longer before coming to rest on the tree top.

i wrap my talons around a sturdy branch and bask in the golden white light. The wind begins to blow in the familiar rhythm of the Universe; gently left, then gently right. i sway with the wind attuning myself to the rhythm and energy of the Universe, forgotten in the abyss.

As i sway, the wind once again begins to carry "the voice" up to me so that i may hear "You have come back as I told you you could. Be not of despair for the abyss you have created is present only as long as you wish it to be there. You have created it to learn a lesson. It is your choice as to how long and how difficult that lesson will be to learn. It is your choice as to how long you stay in the abyss."

"i do not like this feeling, this abyss. i truly want to get out, to learn the lesson. But how do i do that? It is so dark. My knowledge seems to have deserted me. i can't find my tools, not even a screwdriver" i shouted at the voice.

The voice answered on the winds once again. "The knowledge is always within. When you come from Light, the God-Spark, the darkness will be gone. For you see it is the Light which will absorb the darkness. Darkness can not be driven out or simply removed. It can not exist in the presence of Light. Come from Light and with the Light and the darkness will be absorbed, the abyss will vanish. Tools will become visible, escape possible."

i took off from the tree top and soared into the air. Contemplating this wisdom as i glided on the currents. The Puzzle Master's voice i now heard calling me back. Reluctantly i turned for the window knowing i must return. i landed softly back in the "window room."

Always so hard to get back in my body after transmuting into the Eagle. Slowly feathers disappeared, replaced by arms and legs, fingers and toes. The weight of my body returned and i could feel the table beneath my back. Hard to stand, to coordinate my movements. Where are my feet? Remember the light!

Driving home from the Puzzle Master's i wondered if i could actually do this; find the Light, climb from the abyss, confront MBO. i heard the Puzzle Master lending support. i heard a Friend with encouragement saying "I'll be here for you." i felt the Eagle begin to rise inside. The oak sapling making his presence known as well. Perhaps, just perhaps i can do this. But i must do it now before my courage fails.

i called MBO when i arrived home and she said "Come now. I have the time to talk."

On the way there i kept surrounding myself with white Light. i opened my Heart so as to come from that place of Love and Light. As i was driving i looked up and saw a hawk circling above the car. Close enough to an Eagle i thought. i saw it as a sign sent by the Puzzle Master and the Universe that things would be alright. i took a deep breath and told myself that i could do this. The Light began to shine; the abyss disappeared.

Nervous but confident i talked to MBO. i told her

> that i couldn't stay. That i had to follow my Heart on what was for my highest good; and at the moment that was being with the Puzzle Master. There was no yelling, no screaming, no "how could you do this?" It was the best of the scenarios i had envisioned in my mind. At the end of our hour long conversation i thanked her for all that she had taught me. i hugged her goodbye as i surrounded us in Light and Love.

I found that day that the past does not equal the present or the future. Only if I chose to carry the past into the present does it appear in the "now." Each and every "now moment" is filled with endless possibilities. I; as the director of this movie called "my life" can lend my thoughts which are energy to any one of these possibilities. I can choose to recreate the next frame exactly as the frame before. Or in that nanosecond between frames where all possibilities exist; I can choose a different scene; just as a movie fades from one shot to the next.

One can not solve a problem with the same mind set which created it. My thoughts of "I can't get out of this situation" only kept me there. It is like the old saying "Whether you think you can or can't, you are right." It was the changing of my perception from "I can't to "I can" that got me out of the abyss. Instead of darkness I chose to see the Light. The endless possibilities now illuminated, I could find the way out. And in that illumination i found my "I."

The past does not equal the present or the future, only if you choose so.

Change your perspective; change your mind, and you change your world.

Chapter 30

Journey of the 'Silver Cord'

For most of this lifetime and I am sure past lifetimes, I believed that asking for help in any way was a weakness. I had been of the mindset that "I can do this myself without any ones help." The more I worked with the Puzzle Master and others of like mind, the more I found this to be untrue. We all need "helpers" in our lives.

I was also learning that the Universe and the Angels were waiting to help us, but we had to ask. They, in of themselves, would not interfere in our lives; but once we "ask" they would rush in to honor that request if it was for our highest good. So many times I did not even think to ask. Today was a different story.

December 3, 2003

Dearest Friend, Puzzle Master and Singer of Songs;

How is it that you always find some unique experience for me? Once again I find myself amazed but not surprised by what happens here in this most sacred space you have created. So I will_begin my story, a tribute to your talents.

I lay on the table as needles begin to be placed; golden needles I believe from the feel of their energy. As I lay there I ask for help with connection to God, the Universe, to the Light. Even before the needles are all placed I begin to drift into a dreamlike state. Odd I thought that there are no instructions from the Puzzle Master as I drift farther into this altered state; and then I am gone.

I feel myself rising above the table, through the ceiling and beyond into what appears to be darkness. I look down to see the "silver cord" extending far below me. I hear in the darkness a voice "Your body is safe. It will be there when you return from your journey. Follow your heart to where it leads you. There you will find what you seek."

And so I turned my attention within, to the place where my heart lives, where the God-spark resides. It was from this place that I again asked for help, not with voice but with pure thought. "There is much I need to learn; among the list is fear of asking for help from others, how to receive as well as give. I will start with this."

Even before the thought was complete I found myself surrounded be a "Presence." A Presence without form but a vibration so high I thought I might explode. Slowly my own vibration began to attune to this vibration, at least enough so that I was comfortable within the Presence. This Presence then enveloped me completely and as It did so a feeling of pure Love, like none other that I have ever felt came over me. At the same time I was wrapped in a blanket of white light as if in a hammock. The two ends suspended from above as I was cradled in the middle. And yet the blanket seemed more expansive than all of time and space.

As I lay there surrounded by Love and Light, the faintest glow of distinct energies, Angels perhaps, formed a circle around me. As they continued to materialize I heard with my ears which do not hear the same Voice I heard carried on the wind in the forest, which was not a voice at all. I can only describe it as instant thought transfer from the Presence to me.

What I heard and felt was this, *"There is nothing here which is not of God, which is not of the Light and pure Love. That includes you and your human body below. You find yourself here as you have asked for help. I AM here to honor that request. I AM here always, even before your thoughts materialize. I AM answers your prayers. Yet you must materialize the thought. For I AM here to help not to interfere."*

"See not the asking for help as a weakness or failure but as a strength. It is your perception which makes it so. I have made a promise to you; 'Seek and ye shall find. Ask and it shall be given unto you even as you ask.' I can do nothing until you ask, for in the asking is My answer. The answer is in the question. Asking will lead to answers, answers lead to remembering, remembering leads to awakening. Yet you must be awake and alert for the answer does not always come directly. The answer may be in a song lyric sent be Me to you. Or in the form of another

human being offering help. I send these answers to you in a form you can understand."

"You ask again of giving and receiving. Both are needed to complete the cycle, to sustain each other. One must give in order to make room for receiving and one must receive in order to have more to give. One can not do one without the other or imbalances occur, limiting both. If one continues to give without receiving the vessel becomes empty. If one receives without giving the vessel becomes full and no further receiving can occur. Do you see? Keep balance within your vessel of both giving and receiving. Allow others the joy and pleasure of giving, allow yourself the pleasure of receiving. Allow your vessel to be filled."

The Voice continued "Remember that you are perfect and whole in Reality. It is only in the illusion that you have created that you are not. Remember this and awaken. The illusion gone when you Re-remember. Reality waiting when you Awaken."

With that thought the lesson seemed to end. The Presence and the other energies slowly dissipated. I find myself gently being released from the hammock, from the Light; once again suspended in darkness from the "silver cord." I feel the thoughts and the voice of the Puzzle Master now pulling me back towards my human body waiting below. I follow the silver cord as it begins to retract; through the darkness, back to Earth, through the ceiling. I hover above my body which is safe on the table as promised. The cord retracts the final 7 feet and I become one with my body again; inhaling deeply to fill my human lungs.

Upon reflection all I can say is "Whoa! How cool was

that!" I learned so much from the "journey of the cord." The lesson of asking for help as a way to awaken, to learn, to re-remember; not as a form of weakness or failure. It is only weakness and failure if I see it as so. It is a label I and my Ego have placed on it. It is time to peel off that label and throw it away.

Giving and receiving; that I was out of balance. I have limited my own supply of both giving and receiving. If I put the thought, the energy into the Universe that I am unwilling to receive, then the Universe will stop giving. For It does not judge my thoughts as right or wrong. It simply follows the command as a computer; if I put "do not give me anything" in, that is what will come out…"nothing."

Lastly but most important; that I do have a connection with God, with the Universe. All I need do is ask and He is there. Even if I don't ask He is there waiting. That I am never alone. I really didn't have to leave my body, travel to the extension of my silver cord to find Him. For I really didn't find Him there. I was looking FOR what I was looking WITH. I used my "God connection" to find my "God connection." It was in my own backyard all along.

Chapter 31

Square Peg in a Round Hole

I have been seeing the Puzzle Master every week for several months now. Each week it seems my journey through the portal to dimensions beyond the Earth plane occurs more smoothly, more rapidly.

I think it must be the gaining of knowledge on both our parts; the Puzzle Master and I. The Puzzle Master has developed an excellent connection to the Universe, to God. She is a pure vessel through which they work. There is a Universal Knowledge which the Puzzle Master now possess. It comes not from the study of books within walls of brick. It comes from no "pattern" of points learned from another. It is Knowledge which can be gained only from a pure connection to The Source.

She has also gained two new dimensions to her Healing. She is now Singer of Songs and Muse. For along with finding puzzle pieces she also finds one's song. She has found the song that I was born with, the song that I have often forgotten or lost. She has found the notes and taken the time and effort to learn my song. Now she sings it back whenever it is lost.

Shawna and the Puzzle Master are also Muse; a source of inspiration, a guiding genius. For each week she guides my growth, my transformation from caterpillar to butterfly, incredible journeys of learning. She claims she is "Just the person who places needles," but I know she is MORE. She has even gotten me to speak.

As for me; I can not explain how I get through the portal. I wish that I knew so that I could lead others there. For now; I can only impart the Knowledge which I have gained here. Perhaps it is Faith, Trust and a KNOWING that it will occur that propels me through the portal. Each day these seem to grow, get stronger; and as they do, the passage from one dimension to another is quicker, is smoother. I have NO doubt in my mind that this transportation will occur. Now I need but to lay upon the table and I am gone.

On or in these other dimensions, depending on your prospective, I have met teachers and guides in every shape and form. I have learned lessons from Indian Shamans and forest rangers, wolves and rabbits, even trees. This day would be no different; my teacher a "beach bum."

February 14, 2004

Dearest Friend, Puzzle Master, Singer of Songs, Muse;

How different this session has been from our "usual," in more ways than one. I did not bring a story, a sense of failure on my part; homework not completed. Yet what seemed a failure in one way became a success in another. I actually talked to you for the hour in which we had. In some ways it actually felt good to "say" the words. It is as though their release relieved some sort of built up energy waiting to burst through as water behind a dam. The pressure released, the dam now safe. Although I must admit, it feels good to put ink to paper once again.

We began as usual, the taking of the pulses. But here is where a difference now occurred. Almost before the first touch I could feel the portal door begin to open. I waited as the palpation of each pulse opened the portal wider and yet I was also aware that I was still within the Sacred Space you create so adeptly. What is this sensation I thought? It is as though I am in two places at once. I am standing on the beach on one side of the portal and yet I can still hear you, feel your touch, converse with you on the other side of the portal. It is as if you have sent me through the portal and yet come with me at the same time. So it is I hear that wood and water did not show up today. That heart is thready at best. I hear a voice, not of the Puzzle Master, but somewhere between the two portals. "It is important that you be aware of what is happening within your body. Often times it tells you of what is happening and yet you do not hear. So it is that the portal remains open between the physical and the Spiritual so that you may hear."

I find myself lying on the beach as the Puzzle Master places the needles, almost as if it is a dream within a dream. I feel the words of the Puzzle Master as she departs back through the portal, "Journey well my

Friend. I will be here to welcome you home." she says as the portal closes silently behind her.

I am on the beach; waves lapping the shore in their familiar rhythm. "I wonder why it is that I journey to the beach so often" I say to no one in particular but myself.

"Because it represents the Source to you" I hear somewhere behind me. I turn to find what I can only describe as a beach bum; hair long and uncombed, several days beard growth upon his face, shorts and a tee shirt which has seen better days. There was a look of knowing in his clear blue eyes which gave me comfort. "Greetings to you," he said with a smile that illuminated the whole beach. With those words I knew that the teacher had arrived.

"When ever it is that you are troubled, you return here. To that which you feel is home, where you can align once again to the rhythm of the Universe, of God. You and the ocean are as one, for the water which surrounds each of your cells is the same water which resides in the ocean. The rhythm of the waves the same as your heart beat. It is where you feel the Presence deep in your heart and soul" he said.

"Yes, you are right" I replied.

"Let's sit and talk awhile" he said. Two beach chairs and an umbrella were conveniently placed not far from where we stood.

We walked down the beach and sat under the shade of the umbrella. Our chairs facing each other he placed my hands between his own weather worn hands, yet they were soft and kind and loving hands. He began again "What is it that troubles you so deeply?"

I looked deep into his blue eyes. I saw in those eyes

no judgment of my words, thus I had the courage to speak. “More times than not the Puzzle Master finds my wood and water to be lacking or missing. I try so hard to maintain them yet I don’t seem to be able to. I sense anger but I don’t know why. I know there is a lesson here, but I can’t seem to find it, to learn it, for it keeps returning.”

I heard a sigh of sadness escape from his lips. He held my hands tightly in his and I began to feel his energy and love mixing with my own. He began to speak, “The person you are speaking of chooses to be angry. It has nothing to do with you, what you say or what you do. Do you understand? For so long you believed that your Truth was that you were the cause of that anger. You tried to please her, many times to no avail. And so it is that you lost sight of who you were, eventually building armor to protect you from the anger. To use a saying, it was as if you were a square peg being forced into a round hole. Eventually from the constant pushing, the corners of your peg rounded. The hole became slightly bigger and indeed your square peg fit into the round hole. Now over the last few months you have removed yourself from that hole and are restoring the squareness of your peg. The lesson my child is not to allow yourself to be placed back in the hole. This you began to accomplish when you did not beg her to stay, as she was wishing you would. Your Truth now and always has been that your square peg does not belong in the round hole. Do you see?”

“I think I am beginning to” I said. “What of my wood and water” I asked? “Why do they not stay? Why is it that they seem to disappear after the Puzzle Master brings them back each week?”

He released my hands from his and leaned back in his chair. "How is it that you try to keep them?" he asked as if he already knew the answer.

I looked into his eyes as I thought for a moment. "I guess after they return I try to hold on to them tightly so they do not leave again" I said gesturing with my own hands, making a fist held tightly to my heart.

He leaned forward in his chair and opened my clenched fist. Now my open hand, palm up, rested near my heart. "Embrace your wood, your water, even your Truth in this manner. In your effort to keep them you have stopped the flow. It is as if you are trying to drink from a straw yet you have pinched it off and wonder why you can not drink. It is the same for your Truth. Hold it lightly with open palm so that that which is Truth may breath. Your fist makes a finite space which limits what it can hold; nothing in and nothing out. Your open palm is infinite in its capacity. Water may now flow freely and wood has the potential to reach the heights of the Heavens. The longer my hand was open the more flow I felt. Stagnant water began to move. The small sapling which had been bent over in my fist now unfolded and stood tall. "Return now with water and wood once again present" he said to me, clasping my hands once more within his, love surging through me.

We rose and began to walk down the beach, the time to return approaching quickly.

"Remember, open palm and no round holes" he said into my ear as he hugged me goodbye.

The portal door appeared and he extended his hand for support as I stepped through. The Puzzle Master was waiting on the other side with a "Welcome home" and a hand as well. For a brief moment I was again in both worlds, connected to the hands of the Puzzle Master and my Spiritual friend. "Peace and Love" were his final words as his hand seemed to disappear through the portal. The door now closed, it is only the Puzzle Master and I in the room.

So I say to you my friends "Never try to put a square peg in a round hole." Although it can be done it is painful. I tried for many, many years to make that peg fit, only to realize that it never belonged there in the first place for that was not its Truth.

The Truth of every peg; no matter its size or shape is that its origin and Truth are Love and Light. That is because each peg is a God-spark, coming from God and the Universe who ARE only Love and Light. One can not be created out of that which it is not. For an apple seed can not grow into an orange nor can a peach grow into an oak tree.

Remember your Truth always. You are Love and Light and Beauty and Happiness. Never let anyone or any thing convince you otherwise.

Chapter 32

Play

Work. It is what the prudent adult does. There are bills to pay, food and clothing to buy for the family, gas for the car. College tuition that you planned on starting to save for when your kids are 5 suddenly is due next month. Sometimes it seems to never end, this thing called work. And so it was for me.

Although I have no children, I had bills none the less. There was the house, the car, food and clothes. There were the boys to feed; Charlie and Emmett; the balls of fur commonly called cats which allowed me to live in "their" house. It seemed that after working three or four nights in a row I was too tired to play. Besides my days off were filled with cleaning and laundry and errands.

And to complicate things I had a bad knee. I had torn a ligament playing softball; twice. A total of ten operations over about 20 years; and I was glad that I could just walk. Playing seemed beyond my capability. My little friend had other ideas.

February 21, 2004

Dearest Friend; Puzzle Master, singer of Songs, Muse;

How unique these last two journeys have been. On my last journey there was the momentary feeling of being in two places at once, both sides of the portal. This week it was as if the portal remained open and there was free movement between the two. Although I must admit that it is a challenge to at be in both places at once as you will see. Somehow thought I think that I will be given the opportunity to practice.

I lay upon the table and await the taking of the pulses, the signal for the portal to open. I close my eyes and the portal is there, waiting for that first touch to open its door. As the Puzzle Master begins the ritual there is the most extraordinary energy I feel passing between her hand and mine. It is intense, magnified, surging to the rhythm of the Universe. I was concentrating on the energy when I hear a voice; the voice of a child. "Come on, the door is open. I've been waiting for you."

I turn to see a girl about the age of 7 or 8; light brown hair and green eyes. She looks familiar but I do not recognize her. Then I hear the Puzzle Master say something about the heart.

"It's okay," the girl says. "I can wait. You talk to the Puzzle Master. I'll wait for you here." She sits in the door jam of the portal.

I hear the Puzzle Master continue saying my heart pulse was running backwards. Guess I better have that checked out I thought. "Indeed you must" I heard from somewhere deep within the portal.

I feel someone next to me and see that my new "friend" is now standing next to me. She is holding my other hand as the Puzzle Master continues the taking of the pulses. "I'm suppose to say 'Greetings' but I like 'Hi' better, so 'Hi! Come on let's go. You can leave your body here while the Puzzle Master finishes. It will remember what she says. Come on let's go!" she says as she pulls on my arm. We walk hand in hand through the portal. I look over my shoulder and see the Puzzle Master continuing to take pulses and start to place needles in my physical body. How very strange to be in two places at once.

As we walk through the portal we are presented with a park. Grass so green it hurts your eyes. Trees and flowers abound. Musical accompaniment provided by Nature itself, birds singing and the chatter of squirrels as they chase each other up trees. There are swings, a teeter-totter, monkey bars; all the things a park should have. My little friend takes off running, arms spread like wings, making the noises of an airplane as she zig zags across the grass.

"Come on," she says, "Don't just stand there."

"But I can't run anymore," I say. "Bad knees"

She comes running over to me and grabs my hand once again. "Not here you don't. Here you can run forever." She tugs on my hand to get me started.

My first few steps are tentative as I wait for the pain but to my surprise there is none. With each step I now pick up speed. To my joy and wonderment I find myself running at full speed, arms spread, making airplane noises as we chase each other through the park. After awhile we tire of running. We both fall upon the grass and just lie there, enjoying the prickling sensation of the grass poking through our clothes.

"Wasn't that fun" she says. "Let's go swing." We gather ourselves up off the grass and head for the swings. She takes the left and I take the right. We sit in the swing, pedal backwards and take off, pumping our legs for all they are worth. Soon we are swinging in synchronization to a rhythm which is familiar to me. Yes, the rhythm of the Universe I thought.

As we swing side by side she begins to speak with the voice of a child but there is a tone of wisdom far beyond her years. It is only then that I realize she is my teacher for this journey. I listen intently as she begins. "I saw you playing in the rain the other day. I was beginning to wonder if you were ever going to come out and play again. We used to play all the time and then one day you went inside and never came back out. Well, maybe a couple of times you came out but you never stayed long. I have seen you jump in mud puddles and for the briefest moments I thought you might stay. But then you went back inside almost before the water hit the sidewalk. Why don't you stay and play any more?"

"Well it's kind of a long story and I'm not sure you would understand" I said forgetting who I was talking with.

"I have all the time in the world" she said. "And I understand more than you can imagine."

"Well I guess I sort of forgot how to play. It seems that even as a kid I was doing adult things; taking care of the house, watching my sisters, that sort of thing. I guess in my child's mind I thought I was being punished for playing, that I wasn't suppose to play any more. So I 'played' sports, my outlet. Then when I hurt my knee I didn't know what else to do. I guess I did go inside after that both physically and mentally. Now it has been so long that I think I have forgotten how to play."

"You're so silly" she said with a laugh that only a child possesses. Its sound made me smile. "God would never punish you for playing. He only wants you to be happy and if playing makes you happy then He is all for it. God is the one who put the fun in play. But it is up to you to find it."

"What about my knee?" I asked. "I don't understand why it happened."

"It was a contract you made with yourself before you incarnated. It was a blessing you gave yourself just as was your sprained ankle. It was the way you chose to slow down so that you could do the inner work to bring you where you are today. There is more that you will learn, more that you and the Puzzle Master must do, more to accomplish before this lifetime is finished. And you will learn to play again. Come on. Let's go to the teeter-totter."

We both jumped out of the swing and headed for the teeter-totter. Up and down we went. How much fun to be up in the air. I asked as we alternated being first up then down, "How do I play now? Adults can't play like kids."

"And why not" she said. "You can still jump in puddles, blow bubbles, laugh, have a snow ball fight. That little girl is still inside you. Ask her. She knows how to play. She will tell you if you will only listen. Take her with you whenever you play and you will never be alone. Don't leave her inside so long next time. I miss her" she said with tears in her eyes.

"Can I ask you a question"

"Sure"

"How is it that you know so much?" I asked. "And you never told me your name."

"I know only as much as you do" she said. "I thought you had recognized me by now."

I looked at her closely. She was familiar but I could not place her in my memory.

It was then that she looked at me with that same wisdom in her eyes and said "I AM YOU!"

She ran from the teeter-totter and grabbed me. I lifted her off the ground, hugging her close to my heart as her legs wrapped around me. She whispered in my ear "I love you, you silly goose."

"I love you too" I said as she jumped back down on the ground. "The Puzzle Master is calling, I have to go now."

We walked hand in hand back through the portal. There waiting for me was the Puzzle Master with a comforting "Welcome back." I returned to my body as my friend continued to hold my hand, the Puzzle Master on the other side taking my pulses once again.

"Bye. Peace and Love to you. Thanks for playing again. Don't be gone so long next time" she said as she waved goodbye. She stepped through the portal and it closed behind her.

Play is so very unique in what it provides. For when you take that little boy or girl with you, you get to play in the world of endless potential. The place where a box can be a space ship or a pirate ship just because you believe it is. Where yellow leaves become a leprechaun's pot of gold. Or the tile on the kitchen floor becomes a highway to every where and any where. The place where everything is possible.

In every day life, play. Play in the world of endless potential. For it is here that dreams and wishes are born. It is here in the potential that all exists, that all is possible. It is from here that Microsoft, Amazon.com and Einstein's Theory of Relativity came.

What lies in your endless potential?

Chapter 33

East Meets West

Since before even meeting Shawna and the Puzzle Master I have and still do sometimes, struggle with blending my knowledge of this wonderful Eastern philosophy and that of Western philosophy and its medicine.

As a nurse practitioner in an intensive care unit, Western medicine is a part of my every day life. Pathophysiology and technology are the basis of my practice; the kidney works a certain way, as well as the intestines and heart. Machines monitor every biological function. I look at thousands of numbers a day which "tell" me the condition of the little Master which visit the unit each day. They tell me every thing from the sugar content of their blood to how well the breathing machine is working. I look at x-rays to determine the condition of their lungs. I prescribe medications to help with every thing from nutrition to blood pressure and all conditions in between. Yet there is a part of me which "sees and feels and senses" more than mere numbers.

Sometimes I call it a gift; yet this day in March I call it a curse. For you see over the nearly 30 years that I have worked in this environment, the little ones and I have formed a special way of communicating. It is not a communication of words but of "Heart-space" to "Heart-space" pure thought. From here I can often hear and see and feel their joy, their pain and their distress. At times I can ask, in this space of Love, "What is it that you need?" and they will tell me. "Breathe faster for me," "Breathe deeper for me," or "It is time for me to go now. Please stop all that you are doing."

It is not a gift I was ready to share with the world, especially my Western colleagues, who believed almost exclusively "in the numbers." Yet the nurses were different. They were not so concerned with numbers as helping to make the babies well. And so it was with this group, that on occasion, I would let down my guard. They began to call me "The Baby Whisperer;" not a name I would choose for myself; for any crying child seemed to calm immediately once placed in my arms. If unable to be held, I could place me hands on the infant and accomplish the same calmness within them. Nurses would appear at my office door requesting "Please come do that 'thing' that you do. This baby will not stop crying." I spent many nights fluctuating between East and West. Yet this night; it was as if I were trying to mix oil and water for there was no mixing, no fluctuating; there was only a crisis within my Being.

<u>March 15, 2004</u>

Dearest Friend, Puzzle Master, Singer of Songs, Muse;

This morning was a spiritual crisis for me. I didn't know what to do with the experience I had just had, but I knew that I could not deal with it alone. I knew some how I had to get to you; first as Friend, second as the Puzzle Master. I walked into my house and collapsed into my chair.

I buried my head in my hands and cried to the Universe, to God "I don't understand this. Why is it that you let me hear these words of the Little Ones, of the little Masters, yet I can not Honor them. Please I beg of You, let Shawna have time for me today. I need the Wisdom which she possesses. I need the comfort and safety of her most sacred space. Most of all I need her Friendship, her kind and loving heart to wrap around these tears. "Please...Help...Me!"

I picked up the phone and dialed. "Does Shawna have an opening today? At 12? Yes. Please put me in. Thank you so much." I said as I replaced the phone in its cradle. "And thank you God for hearing my prayer" I choked through tears which would not stop.

At last it was noon. You gifted me with love and a hug as I entered. It was your Friendship and love which made me feel safe enough to tell my story. A story that no one else would understand or believe for that matter. So I began to tell you of seeing fear in young Max's eyes as he "told" me of things not going as he planned. Of seeing directly into his Soul through his eyes. Of my hands not being my own as I helped the next one breathe. Of another little one who thanked me for putting in a breathing tube because she was so tired. You understood. You didn't call me crazy or weird or an idiot. You understood. You understood. My Heart and Spirit filled with gratefulness, with Love for that understanding.

My story continued with the next little one; telling me of her wish to not have a breathing tube replaced. I told you of how I could not honor her wish for I was bound by Earth Laws to replace it. Each time I would try I could only hear her pleading "Please leave it out. I am tired and want to just go home." I was unable to place the tube as I listened to her plea, although I tried several times. I had to give the tube to the doctor to place.

The retelling of this story brought tears to my eyes. I could barely speak around the lump which formed in my throat. I fought hard to keep the tears at bay, to keep them in check. Then I heard "It's okay to let them go." Those words felt so safe, coming from you my Friend. I wanted to hug you, to say thank you for the gift of tears, for the safe sanctuary that you provided for them, but I was bound to the chair and all I could do was let the tears continue.

My story told, it was now time for the Puzzle Master. I rose from my chair and moved slowly to the table. It was a struggle to stay there while I waited for the taking of the pulses; yet I knew that what you found I needed to hear; hear with my human ears. And so it is that I heard that the "Husband and Wife Split" had occurred. This has happened once before I remember, some time ago. I remembered it had to do with conflict between two opposites. I had to smile to myself. The pulses always tell the truth.

I heard the voice of the Puzzle Master "I must treat the split first. Then you will go on what ever journey you need to go on." I could struggle to stay no longer; having heard what was necessary. I was through the portal before a single magic needle was placed.

I found myself floating from my silver cord suspended in darkness. Once again as in my last journey, there was no visible portal through which I stepped. I simply arrived here. Indeed the Puzzle Master has acquired more talent; has risen to some new level. For now she sends me directly to my destination, no need for a portal. I do love to watch her grow; to watch her progress as Healer; it gladdens my Heart. I remain in awe of how quickly her talents have progressed and remain humbled to accept the benefits of her ever growing talent.

As I lay suspended in the darkness, strands of light begin to weave beneath me. I watch as they form a hammock of sorts; one that I have seen before. The weaving complete it feels as if hands of pure Love gently place me within the hammock. The hammock folds around me, cradling me within the Light. The hammock begins to sway back and forth as a mother rocks her child. It sways to the rhythm of the Universe, of God. It is comforting and safe here. The same feeling as the Puzzle Master's Sacred Room.

As I lay in the hammock rocking back and forth, Beings of Light begin to surround me. Words without sound begin to float on the silence to directly to my ears.

"Greetings child. We have heard and felt your words of distress and despair. We bring you Love and Compassion from the Father. We are here to answer your request for help. How is it that We may serve you?"

"I don't understand what is happening. How is it that I arrive here without going through a portal? Why is it that I hear the cries of children yet I can not honor their wishes? What good does it do to hear them if I can't help them?" I cried, tears streaming down my face.

A finger of Light reached out and wiped the tears from my cheek. I watched as the tears were absorbed into the Light and vanished. In their place a blanket of Love appeared and wrapped itself around me. Words began to flow again in the Silence.

"Here in this dimension, at this vibration, you will understand that which We will say to you. You will remember it as it is Truth. Your journey through the portal has been a process. It is as with mathematics on your plane. You must start with adding and subtracting before you can do calculus. You and the Puzzle Master have progressed over time, each helping the other. Together you began with first finding the portal, though it took some time to find it at first. You then progressed to less and less time needed to pass through the portal. And now because of your journeys together, the portal remains open; as it always was. For in Reality it was never closed. Now you KNOW and therefore do not need to SEEK. Do you understand?"

"Yes, I believe that I do. Thank you" I replied. "But what of the little ones?" I asked.

"Yes the little ones" They said. The Light got brighter just at the thought of the little ones. "Can you not see how you have helped each other?"

"No. It only seems that I failed them." I countered.

"Look again," They replied.

I saw the events of the night replayed somewhere in

my mind's eye. After it was over, a new film started. It had no title, only a date; NOW. I saw that Max was not as frightened now. He was grateful to know that he could leave. He had talked to his parents and although it was painful and heartbreaking for them, they seemed to understand his wishes. There would be no more interventions. I saw them disconnect wires and tubes; dress him in a little baseball outfit and wrap Max in a blanket. They were going home. They were going to spend their final moments together, as a family, at home. Max was happy with this decision.

Next was little Sabaa. She had been the one who had pleaded with me not to put her breathing tube back in. She was next to me now, yet I could see her physical body still lying in her incubator. We talked for what seemed like hours. We understood each other after that "conversation;" both of us more at peace now. Sabaa just wanted someone to acknowledge her cry, acknowledge that she had wishes. She understood that the Earth Laws compelled me to replace the tube. She told me that she had decided to stay a few days longer now that the tube was back, because of her father. He loved her so.

Max and Sabaa faded back into the dimension from which they came. The Beings of Light broke the silence "And so it was that you did not fail. You heard them and one must HEAR their Spiritual voices before one can DO for them. Have patients my child. The doing will come in time. It is the first step; it is enough for now that you were able to hear them. And you did affect them even though you could not see it at that moment."

The blanket of Love was slowly pulled back. The

end of my journey nearing.

"One last thing," the Beings of Light said to me. "The little ones have left you a present."

I looked all around for a box or an envelope but found nothing. "Look here," They said.

I looked above my head and saw a mirror, in it a reflection of myself. To my amazement a large chunk of my breast plate armor was missing. "But how?" I asked.

The reply from the Beings of Light floated on the Silence "Your tears of Love and Compassion for the little ones has melted it away. It is their gift to you for listening to them."

"How can I ever thank them, and Shawna and the Puzzle Master for all that everyone has done?" I asked.

"Continue your journey; continue your quest to bloom and fly. Continue your journey to the mountain top. And once there remember to let go. Peace and Love to you child."

With those parting words I was gently removed from the hammock. The Puzzle Master's comforting words of "Welcome home" wrapped around me as I lay once again safe upon the table.

One does not always know how their "presence" will affect another Beings life. Little did I know at the time that Max and Sabaa wished merely to be "heard." That no "doing" was required from me, only the simple act of "Being" with them. It was compassion for their spirits which they desired. They helped me to re-remember a philosophy I had heard long ago; "Just because we can doesn't mean we should." It is a phrase I use now with my Western colleagues. More times than not, they actually seem to understand it's meaning.

The Little Masters gifted me with assistance in my growth that day. Their "presence" affected my life as well. They allowed me to express compassion towards them; resulting in a loosening of "the reigns" as it were for me. The gift of tears too long held back. The additional gift of melting armor.

The combining of East and West still remains a challenge for me at times. It seems that the more I acknowledge that part of me which is intuitive, which is the Baby Whisperer; the more I accept that aspect of me; the better "in tune" I am with the Little Ones and the less I rely on only "numbers".

Neither philosophy has changed, yet each day it becomes easier to combine them. Once I saw them as complementary and not advisories to one other the blending and balancing became much easier. Now they are to me as yin and yang; each contains a part of the other. It is the Little Masters who now draw from this emulsion that which they need; sometimes East and some times West. I am Honored to be of service to them; in either direction or both.

Change your mind and you change your world.

Chapter 34

Be the Teacher

Shawna and my relationship as "Friends" was growing as fast or faster than our relationship as student/teacher or Healer and patient. Over the last several months I had learned of her story, of her life, of the devastation of losing her children. I had held her in my arms on Thanksgiving last while she cried for them. But things were beginning to change.

Her children's father had been very sick with leukemia. He went into the hospital in October of 2003 for treatment. Shawna's sons had been living with their father up until that time; as he insisted he would "never be a part-time parent." Although they shared custody of the boys, they rarely visited her; the oldest far less than his brother.

When Shawna's ex-husband could no longer care for the boys their uncle took over these duties. By the end of

October it was evident that her son's father was not getting any better and could possibly die.

The father's side of the family was not too fond of the youngest boy. He seemed to irritate them in some way. He was not accepted into this "tribe" of his birth. He was an outsider in his own family. His uncle became less and less enchanted with him each day. Finally at the end of October he had had enough. He dropped the boy at Shawna's door step with only a duffle bag full of clothes saying "I don't want him anymore. He is yours now."

Shawna's dream had come true although not in the way she had imagined; but her son was back in her life. Yet it was a major adjustment for her entire "new family" as well as her son. He had essentially been out of her life for many years. He arrived overweight, covered from head to toe with eczema and barely able to breath secondary to asthma. He also had behavior problems and was doing poorly in school. Shawna took the bull by the horns. She got him the medical attention he needed, tutors for school, even a physiatrist to help with his behaviors. There was a lot of adjustment required on every ones part.

I felt a kinship with this boy before I ever met him. Once I did, the feeling was even stronger. And so to help out everyone; Shawna, her son and myself I offered to take him for a weekend once a month. I thought it would be a time that would be focused just on him, to have fun. Besides it would give me a chance to be a "kid" again. But as the first weekend adventure was about to arrive, I panicked.

Old tapes of "You are not good enough" began to surface. I lost all self confidence. I had nothing but self doubt within my being. How could I care for this child that was so precious to Shawna. I felt less than qualified. I turned as always to the Puzzle Master for answers.

<u>March 6, 2004</u>

Dearest Friend, Puzzle Master, Singer of Songs, Muse;

I arrive this day so scared, so full of self doubt, no self worth. I was to be entrusted with your son; he who is most precious to you. He whom you devote your love and life to. And how was it that I, a butterfly who barely had wings, who still struggles with flight; how is it that I was to be Teacher to this Master? Surely I am not qualified yet. I my self can barely fly. I have not learned enough yet. It was only a few days ago that I could not arrange rocks correctly on a plate ("You need more black ones in the front") or choose the right vegetables to go with dinner ("You can't have broccoli and peas"). If I can not even arrange rocks, how can I teach this Master, this Master who will look to me for guidance?

"Oh God I pray for guidance. There is so much at stake here; the Healing of a young Master. I can not bare the thought of failing him or his mother. I come to you with only Love and Compassion in my Heart for this boy and Shawna. I can not do this alone. And so I ask on bended knees to be the Vessel through which Your Light, Your Love and Your Wisdom come. Amen." This is my prayer as I walk to the table, awaiting the opening of the portal.

I lay upon the table and close my eyes. Almost instantly the portal appears, the door is open even before the first pulse is taken. I hear the ocean and its familiar waves outside the portal. A wave rolls gently over the threshold, its crest suspended in mid-air beside me. The tip of the wave undulates up and down, beckoning me. I rise from my body and stand upon the crest as it gently carries me to the shore. I expect to find my beach bum waiting there for me but there is no one; it is only me and the ocean.

I stand on the shore as waves lap at my feet. There is a force now pulling me to enter the water. I begin walking into the ocean having no fear that I will drown as my last journey prepared me well for this one. Totally submerged within the ocean I begin swimming, guided by a force far greater than I. I can feel as I swim the Puzzle Master taking pulses, guiding the placement of needles using this same force. It is a little hard to make my body talk, being in two places at once and one of those being under water. Eventually the words form and are spoken by the physical body left behind. I turn and tread water, watching as wells and springs and rivers of energy are connected in my body still on the Puzzle Master's table. Knowing that it is in good, safe and loving hands I resume my journey.

I hear in the distance the song of the humpback whale. I do not know if it is close or far away. And so I remain suspended within the ocean and wait. Only moments pass before I feel the current change. I look and before me is the most beautiful humpback whale; her child at her side. They come close to me. The mother reaches out with her fin and tenderly brushes it along my body. The two of them then seem to dance, turning and spinning as they sing. The vibration of their song resonates within my Heart; for its notes are of pure Love and Joy.

The dance complete they come to rest before me. It

is the Mother who speaks first. It is not her words which I hear but her thoughts that I feel. "Greetings to you."

"That was such a beautiful dance and an even more beautiful song" I reply. "But how is it that you have come to me here in the middle of the ocean?'

The Mother looks at me with eyes full of emotion, feeling and wisdom and says "You have asked for guidance, for wisdom. We are here to help. You have connected to God, to the Universe. He has sent us as his messengers. The others will be here soon. Let's go to the surface and await their arrival."

We began to swim toward the surface; I of course swimming much slower than the whales. The Mother comes along side of me and says "Climb upon the little one's back and you can ride to the surface."

"But what if I hurt him?"

"You are trusted with all creatures small and vulnerable; human and animal; for we see in your Heart only Love and Compassion for them" Mother answers.

Then the little one speaks with words without sound "I trust you too. Come on it will be fun." And so I climb on his back and the three of us glide toward the surface.

As we break the surface I hear the most incredible noise. Hundreds and hundreds of other ocean creatures arriving at this same exact destination. I hear porpoises and dolphins as they expel water through their blow holes. I hear seals barking as they leap through the ocean. They all gather around us leaving the center of the circle open. The Mother motions for the little one and I to go to the center of the ring. The Mother says only these words "It is your time."

With these words the little one and I dive below the surface. I feel myself being transformed as we dive. A veil of red floats inches above us now. It forms a square six feet by six feet. Suddenly the little one and I are propelled through the red veil at a speed I did not think he was capable of reaching. I closed my eyes as the veil covered me entirely and we surfaced once again in the middle of the circle.

I was now crouched upon his back, my eyes still closed, yet I was also next to the Mother watching myself from afar. I could not believe my eyes. I was crouched, wrapped in wings of red with white tips. As I stood the wings unfolded to reveal red buckskin pants and shirt. A red mask painted around my eyes, a black headdress flowed behind me. I stood tall, wings fully extended and began to dance as a chant escaped my lips. Some how I knew every step, every turn, every spin in this intricate dance. And as I watched the meaning of the movements came flooding back to me; the Rise of the Phoenix. From the ashes of despair come new life, Wisdom.

The dance complete I now stand before all these wondrous creatures. The Mother speaks for them all "It is why we brought you here. So that you could see that Wisdom does exist within you."

I was overwhelmed with feelings of Joy, Love and Compassion sent to me by all of those Godly creatures. "Thank you so much. How can I ever repay you?" I asked.

The Mother swam next to me and our eyes locked. It seemed as if there was a transfer of her Wisdom to me and the answer became clear.

"Be the Teacher" was the unified sound which came

from the entire circle.

I found myself once again on the little one's back, the Mother at our side. We dove in unison back into the ocean and as we did the red veil washed away. I hugged the little one as we headed for the shore. There the wave was waiting for my return. I climbed upon it's crest as we headed for the portal.

"Thank you again" I said waving goodbye to my new friends.

"Peace and Love to you" they both replied.

The wave placed me back on the table and I watched as it receded through the portal. As always the Puzzle Master was waiting for me with a loving "Welcome back."

Nelson Mandela made a speech originally written by Marianne Williamson that addresses this lesson far better than I.

"Our deepest fear is not that we are inadequate. Our deepest fear is that we are powerful beyond measure. It is our light, not our darkness, that most frightens us. We ask ourselves, who am I to be brilliant, gorgeous, talented, and fabulous? Actually, who are you not to be? You are a child of God. Your playing small doesn't serve the world. There's nothing enlightened about shrinking so that other people won't feel insecure around you. We are all meant to shine, as children do. We are born to make manifest the glory of God that is within us. It's not just in some of us, it's in everyone. And as we let our own light shine, we unconsciously give other people permission to do the same. As we are liberated from our own fear, our presence automatically liberates others."

To fear that we have too much power and are not as inadequate as we think? This seems a contradiction to many of us. Our greatest fear is that we are inadequate, helpless and of no consequence in the grand scheme of life. That is our negativity, our EGO, which is self-destructive. The Ego's main function it to keep us from the light, the light which comes from the soul within; the light that we all have. Darkness is fear, the road to self destruction and denial of all our human virtues. If severe enough, it leads to our soul going to sleep for self protection.

I was teacher that weekend, and many weekends and days afterwards. I became aware that "hiding my light under a bushel" did not serve Shawna's son. For it only fostered the darkness, the continued sleepiness of the Soul. It was only by showing my own light that his darkness could be absorbed into that light, that his Soul could "awaken" to its own light.

To use an analogy; think of two candles; one with wick burning the other unlit. In most instances we try to light the other candle by blowing out our own. Funny how that never seems to work. Yet if we make our candle as big and bright as we can manifest from the potential, we can light a million times a million candles and never diminish our own flame. And those millions of candles shall light millions more. And Humanity would AWAKEN.

BE the Teacher! BE the Light! BE all you can BE! BE Awake!

Chapter 35

Darkness Verses Light

The vow taken by my nine year old self of "Never let them see you cry" was not serving my now 50 year old self any longer. Feelings that I had stuffed into a deep dark hole were beginning to make themselves known. Known in physical ways as my digestion was poor, my sleep even worse.

Yet I could not find the source of these ailments; try as I may. The source it would turn out was buried in some cave I had constructed many years ago. A cave I had dynamited closed in hopes that what was inside would never escape. I left the cave unmarked in hopes that I would never have to find it again.

Although I knew not where the cave was; it knew where I was. That which I had buried there had rotted in the darkness. Now it was becoming an abscess which was about to burst forth and poison my entire system.

The Puzzle Master, with the Wisdom of a Sage and the tracking skills of the ultimate guide, began to uncover the trail back to the cave. It was a journey I did not want to take; but knew I must. For Healing does not occur when one has a "pus pocket" inside of them. Magic needles and the 5 Elements became my neutralizers of poison.

May 15, 2004

Dearest Friend, Puzzle Master, Singer of Songs, Muse;

There was fear and some anxiety surrounding this cave. Fear of where it would take me; of the feelings it would bring to the surface, of how to cope with those feelings once the journey was over. Yet it was a journey that must be undertaken. It was your Love and Trust that I wrapped myself in that day as I lay on the table. For I knew that those two things would keep me safe and guide me home.

I lay upon the table wrapped in your Love and Trust, holding it close to me as a child holds their blanket. The taking of the pulses begins. Something about, "Your water is so deep." And then those words which have no sound began.

"Greetings. Indeed water and fear together. That which you fear you have buried so deep. Deep inside of you where it has waited in the darkness hidden, festering into an abscess. Here it waits, hoping that you will remember in your mind that it is here. That is all it needs to maintain its power, just a millisecond of thought towards it. For that is the only way in which it can grow and fester, hidden in the darkest recesses of you, poisoning all other thoughts which come close to it. Now is the time, before it destroys you entirely. Take our hand and we shall guide you."

I looked to the side and saw the portal, a few more particles of golden dust adhering to the jam. A hand of golden white light reached out for mine.

"Come my child. Take my hand." I reached for the hand and it propelled me through the portal at lightening speed.

"I can not breathe," I heard my human voice say. The speed so swift I could not catch my breath.

"Remember you are only an observer," I heard in the distance. The comforting voice of the Puzzle Master still with me.

I tried to relax, knowing that my body was safe on her table but my lungs did not seem to fill. There was no light and a feeling of falling, falling deep into the darkest darkness that I had ever experienced.

"Please," I begged, "Make it stop."

I began to slow down as if brakes were being applied to some wild carnival ride. Finally a full breath filled my lungs as the ride came to a halt and I was gently released.

I caught my breath for a few moments and then felt the urge to run. But where do I run to? It is so dark and I can not see. I put my hands in front of me as I feel for obstacles and begin to walk. Yet as I walk my breath becomes labored again.

"Where is this place? Why am I here?" I ask of no one in particular.

Words with no sound begin again, "Running will not restore the light or your breath. It only robs you of that which you now seek. It is impossible to run away here."

Almost having no choice, my breath now coming in short staccato bursts, I stop. I collapse on what must be the ground. Waves of nausea course through my body as I pull my knees to my chest and begin to rock. As each wave crests the retching begins. The taste of bile travels up and down my throat.

"What is happening to me? What is this place?" I ask again.

The Voice returns. "This is the dark hole which you have dug to hide your feelings. Always digging deeper and deeper. It took many years to construct. You placed these feelings here and then abandoned them. Here in this darkness, hidden from view, they began to fester. Now after so long they have caused an abscess of sorts, poisoning you from the inside out. It is time to access this abscess, to drain it of its poison. You can feel how it sickens you. That which is buried here must rise to the surface, for it is the light which will stop its growth, which will neutralize the poison."

"These feelings are so painful. The memories which accompany them so intensely painful. It feels as if my entire being is being ripped apart. I beg you to let me keep these painful feelings buried. I do not think I can survive the reliving, the re-feeling of the memories. Please take this pain from me or let me die." I cried as yet another wave a nausea swept over me.

"You will survive," the Voice proclaimed. "The process of healing has already begun just by you finding where the feelings have been hidden. It is the first step in bringing them to the surface, to the Light. The first step in neutralizing and relieving the pain."

"But it still hurts. The pain so intense," I cried once again as now vomit tries to spew from my mouth yet I swallow it down.

"Do not swallow your feelings down. Do not return them back to the black hole where they will continue to poison you. Let them spew forth where they will be transformed by the Light," the Voice replied.

Vomit again tried to spew from my mouth. My throat burned as if liquid fire was trying to escape. Yet I could not let it out and swallowed it down.

The Voice rang out, "What was the feeling that you just swallowed down? Give it a name. It is the second step in your Healing process. You can not Heal the unknown, only the known."

I could barely speak now between the pain and the fire in my throat. These were the words which I heard escape from my mouth. "I am unworthy and unlovable. To Love and be Loved in return is all I ever wanted. I have all this Love inside and have tried to give it away. I seem to only get pain in return, at least until recently. I gave the key to my Heart to the taxi driver. He gained access to my Heart only to rip it from my body and stomp it into the ground with words of 'You are not good enough. You can do nothing right. You should feel privileged that I even go out with you.'

After that I put my wounded Heart back inside and tried to keep it from dying. I tried to revive it with the 'flower man.' He thought that giving me dinner and flowers 'entitled' him to 'dessert' at my expense. This time not only my Heart but my Soul were violated. He ripped them to shreds, almost beyond recognition. Somehow the Essence of my Heart survived that attack, I know not how." I had to stop momentarily as another wave of nausea swept through my body.

"Continue my child. I am with you," the Voice encouraged.

I took a deep breath and began again, "It is the Essence of my Heart which still needs to give and receive Love today. I am amazed by its struggle to survive after all that has happened. How damaged it has become. Yet it is the Love of a True Friend which is helping it to survive at present. I know not why she tends to this damaged and unworthy ember, but I am glad that she does." I could speak no more as exhaustion set in.

With these words spoken the pain began to subside to a more tolerable level. The fire in my throat cooled. There was a crack in the darkness and golden white Light began to seep in. I uncurled slightly from my fetal position; sat up and shielded my eyes from the bright light. The light filtered through the crack like fog on a misty day. It swirled about as a small tornado might do, a twisting funnel now near my feet. Slowly the swirling fog began to take on a familiar form, yet it was pure energy, pure Light. Arms of Light reached out and scooped me from the floor; cradling me close to what would be the Light Beings Heart.

The Voice spoke with kindness and love, "You have undertaken much this day. The Healing process has begun. Know that you ARE worthy and you ARE Loved. Know that the dark is not of God for He is Absolute Light and Love. Darkness only continues the process of 'festering.' For in the Light; all is Whole, Beautiful, Pure, and Perfect, as it ALWAYS has been and ALWAYS will be. Swallow feelings no more. Allow them to spew forth into the Light and poison you no more. Fear not my child."

I hear the Puzzle Master calling me home. I find my blanket of Love and Trust and wrap it tightly around my hurting exhausted body. The Light Being replaces me gently on the table.

"Peace and Love to you my child. Remember I AM with you always," and it vanished. I awaken on the table; a wave of nausea crashes over me. "Swallow no more," I hear in the background and I run for the bathroom, allowing the feelings to come forth into the Light.

A university professor challenged his class "Did God create everything?"

A student replied, "Yes."

The professor continued; "If God created everything, then He created evil too. And since our works define who we are, then God is evil."

The class became silent.

Suddenly another student raised his hand and asked, "Professor, does darkness exist?"

The professor responded, "Yes."

The student replied, "No, sir, darkness does not exist. Darkness is just the absence of light. Light, we can study, but not darkness. In fact, we can use Newton's prism to break the white light into many colors and study the various wavelengths of each color. But you cannot measure darkness. A simple ray of light can break into a world of darkness and illuminate it. How can you know how dark a certain space is? You measure the amount of light present. Darkness is a term used by man to describe what happens when there is no light present." Then the young man asked, "Sir, does evil exist?"

Now uncertain, the professor responded, "Of course."

To this the student replied, "No, evil does not exist, sir, or at least it does not exist unto itself. Evil is simply the absence of God." It is just like darkness, a word that man has created to describe the absence of light. God did not create evil, it is the result of what happens when man does not have God's love present in his heart. Evil is like the cold that comes when there is no heat, or the darkness that comes when there is no light."

The professor sat down. The young student's name was Albert Einstein.

Chapter 36

Forgiveness

A little more than a year had passed now since I first meet Shawna and the Puzzle Master. Many changes had taken place; much growth had occurred on both our parts.

Shawna seemed to grow stronger as a Healer every day. Her connection to the Universe, to God becoming more pure. She was able to connect to the "Source," to the place were Universal Knowledge resides. And it was from here, this place of Knowledge, that she obtained the lesson plans for my journeys. For the needle patterns that she used were not of the text books of this Earthly realm, but from the realm of Divinity.

She was also able to send me through the portal instantaneously.

As for me; my journeys were becoming more

"advanced." Now not only was I transported through one portal, but often there would be a second. The vibration behind this second veil much higher than the first. A dimension I could not even imagine existed just a few short months ago.

In the beginning I seemed to have many "guides" on my journeys. They came in all shapes and sizes, from Indians, to whales, to trees. It mattered not the form they took for they always introduced themselves with the same phrase "Greetings to you." It was the signal that the lesson was about to begin.

Always during our session there were many "visitors" present. Sometimes they were Light Beings, others would be balls of color bouncing around the room, even angels came to visit. The last few sessions there was a Being who seemed to be a return visitor.

He had been present now for the last three sessions. He stood in the background, mostly observing I think. I called him "the man in blue" for he always appeared in royal blue clothes. This day he would do more than observe.

June 9, 2004

Dearest Friend, Puzzle Master, Singer of Songs, Muse;

There are many visitors with us this day. It seemed the whole room was full. How grateful I am to all who come to lend their support and protection. It seems as though I would need them all. I could feel the fear within me building. Yet there was one which stood out and you saw him too. He was standing next to the candle dressed in royal blue. He had dark hair and eyes the color of the Earth. His spirit was kind and gentle.

He seemed familiar to me but I could not remember from where.

It is with apprehension that I approach the table. This day you ask "If I had a magic wand what would you want?"

I replied, "To regain my power."

I sense that this will involve going back in time, perhaps several lifetimes. The memories unleashed from the cave still fresh in my mind, still painful. Yet I know that leaving them buried will not serve me.

As the taking of the pulses begins I am again aware of the man in blue by the candle. He is so familiar yet I can not place him. As I watch a staff appears in his hand and his color changes from blue to purple. I recognize him now. He is the same man who escorted me into the Court, the Court of Acceptance, low those many months ago.

"I will protect you and guide you on your journey," he said. "Do not be afraid. You are only here to observe. I will be by your side, now as always. I shall be waiting for you across the portal." He faded and then disappeared.

I was very aware during the taking of the pulses. This was the first time that I almost do not want to go through the portal. Fear of the known as well as the unknown keeps the urge to leave low. Yet I want to get through this, willing to do what ever it takes. There are two pulses on my left wrist which when touched sent energy shock waves through my arm. The middle deep pulse sent waves of energy to my elbow which then returned and blew out my little finger. The superficial pulse next to my thumb sent a tingling sensation to my back below my shoulder blade. I will have to ask the

Puzzle Master of this on my return.

The Puzzle Master begins to place needles and the portal beckons. Many needles seem to be placed around my heart. My hope is that they will protect it from all that it is about to encounter.

I hear the Man in Blue calling me, "It is time to go, to begin your journey. Take my hand and I will guide you."

It is with great reluctance that I rise from the table. It is only because I trust you implicitly Puzzle Master that I now venture through this portal. You said it will be okay. I trust you and so I step through the portal ready to face whatever is on the other side.

As I step through the Man in Blue is waiting. He took my hand and held it tight. "Greetings," he said. "I have been sent to guide you on this journey. I shall keep you safe. You are only the observer here. Please remember that." His voice was so kind. His Earthy brown eyes so Loving and Wise. I felt more at ease now with him at my side.

We began walking a dirt path; flowers of every variety on either side as far as one could see. No words were spoken as we walked hand in hand through this glorious splendor, yet I could feel his energy coursing through me. We came to a bench and sat down facing each other. He reached into the front pocket of his cloak and produced several pictures.

"These pictures will help you remember. Look at them as the observer, a step removed, not as participant. It is the way to forgive, to heal. Shall we begin?"

"Okay," I said with a touch of reluctance in my voice.

He showed me a series of four pictures. The first

was one of myself, a boy of three or four and a man; my husband, standing outside a cottage. Then there was one of me inside a horse drawn wooden box being driven down a road. The next was of me in a stockade and the last was of me 'burning at the stake.' The memories came flooding back; the terror, the horror of it all. The betrayal that I felt.

"Observer only," he said as he held my hands. "You need not experience the heat of the flames or the terror of the cage again. The townspeople were afraid. They feared what to them was the unknown; bottles of strange fluids, chants and incantations. You can not understand their fear as Healing was known to you. Known to you from long before even this lifetime. Fear and love cause people to do very irrational things sometimes. It was not you personally that they came to destroy but you as 'symbol' of fear of the unknown. As Jesus said 'Forgive them for they know not what they do.' Can you find it in your Heart to forgive them? Know that that fear does not exist today."

"So it wasn't 'me,' it was Fear? That's why they killed me?"

"Yes," he said. "Know that your son went on to become a great Healer. Had you not died he would have chosen differently. He did it out of Love for you and he helped many people." That image brought tears to my eyes.

He next showed me pictures of a yellow cab and then one of a book. The cab I recognized immediately and all that went with it yet I could not remember a book which went with this scenario. He must have sensed my confusion as he began to speak, "You know of the man who drove the cab yet you do not understand the significance of the book? Is that correct?"

"Yes," I said. "I remember well what I endured with him. But I don't remember any book."

"Yes, I understand," he said as if in answer to guidance only he could hear. He held my hands in his and I felt the vibration rise. He began taking deep breaths and the energy rose yet again. I followed his breathing with my own. We were surrounded in golden white light; the gardens ceased to exist. He now spoke to me in a voice which had no words for words were not needed here. Here was Truth; here was Knowingness; here was Understanding.

He began, "We have brought you here to this space, to this vibration so that you may re-remember. Re-remember why it is that you chose this lesson. We have brought you here so that you may Understand. This Understanding will lead to Forgiveness. It is the path to eliminate pain and suffering."

I looked at him and saw a glow around him, separate from the golden white light which surrounded us. I looked into his wise earthy brown eyes and Knew that only Truth could reside here in this space. He continued with his words of Wisdom.

"There were many reasons that you chose this lesson; only one of which was to learn that you could reclaim yourself. You had a much more compassionate reason as well. You chose this lesson as part of a contract; a very special 'Contract of Compassion' between you and another. In what you would call the recent past you rediscovered a writing by your philosopher Nietzsche which read 'To understand another person is to imitate their feelings in ourselves.'

It resonated with the very core of you, with your Soul. It was and is the basis of your 'Contract of Compassion.' You too endured loss of self esteem and almost total destruction of your Who. Feelings that you endured in yourself so that you could understand another. Understand from a place of compassion. That experience provided some insight into feelings and emotions about another's life that you were destined to meet many years later. Her name this lifetime is Shawna as you know. It is the how and why that you can write her book. It is this 'Contract of Compassion' which you made for her which has bonded you two together in this lifetime as well as others. Do you remember now?"

He sat closer to me and hugged me as I cried. "I remember. I understand now. I truly understand now," I said through my tears.

"All those years lost hating myself, hating him. Now I see that he assisted me in being able to see and feel first hand, if even on a smaller scale what Shawna felt. He gave me insight into those feelings so that I could tell her story for her as Nietzsche said. It is because of this experience that I can help her with her greatest wish; to tell her story to her children in hopes they too will understand. I forgive him. I have no hate for him; because now …I Understand."

We held each other tightly as the golden white light faded, the vibration lowered and the gardens returned, the glow around him now almost gone.

"How can I ever thank you?" I asked.

He just looked at me with his wise eyes and said, "Write her book. That will be thanks enough."

"I promise. If it takes my last breath, it will be

written. That is a promise to Shawna as well as to you," I said.

We hugged again, energy surging through us. He walked me back to the portal as the Puzzle Master was calling me home. He lead me over the threshold and helped me back on the table. I told him "Thank you. Thank you for everything."

He turned to leave and I asked, "Who are you?"

He looked at me with loving eyes and said, "That is better left to another time. We will meet again I promise. Peace and Love to you." With that said he vanished beyond the portal.

"All truths are easy to understand once they are discovered; the point is to discover them." Galileo

"If you want to understand today you have to search yesterday." Pearl S. Buck

"To understand everything is to forgive everything." Buddha

This is what the Man in Blue, the Puzzle Master and her magic 5 Element needles taught me this day. For truth and understanding were locked in a cave I had abandoned long ago. I did not recognize that the absence of Light; darkness; only kept the truth hidden. That this darkness was a "trick," an illusion used by the Ego. An illusion that I believed because I was "asleep." With eyes closed, I could not see the Light.

And so on my journey back to yesterday I understood today. I understood how I had recreated each new frame of the present from the past. How I had merely placed today's date on all those frames of the past and called it "the present."

Now more awake, in the presence of Light, I understood. I understood and I was able to forgive. For I saw that once again, that which seemed to be a tragedy in the dark was a Blessing in the Light. I had an understanding of what Shawna went through. I had walked at least half a mile in her shoes. And because of this, I am able to write her story from my Heart as well as hers. To paraphrase Nietzsche "I now understand another person because I imitated her feelings in myself." I would not hesitate to make that "Contract of Compassion" again.

Today, in 2006, I no longer waste time hating "taxi man" and "flower man" for now that I am more awake I see the Blessing that they were in my life. It was I who chose the difficulty of the lesson; they were merely as characters in a play; a play entitled "My Life."

Chapter 37

Fruits of the Cave

The next few weeks were difficult after visiting the cave of "hidden feelings." I was not as "awake" as I am now. There were days that I wish I had never found that cave, and there were days that I was glad that I did. Both the cave and the light seem to come with pain, sorrow and a sadness; each for different reasons. The cave contained the feelings of less than, of verbal abuse, of not good enough; while the Light contained unfulfilled dreams and wishes. I knew how to deal with the cave, for now I understood it. But I didn't know how to deal with the things of the Light, the dreams, the wishes.

With all those feelings locked in the cave it was much easier to "pretend" that I needed no one but myself. Now that they were in the Light I could no longer pretend. Where once I avoided human contact, I now miss it. I so cherish the hugs I received each week from my Friend Shawna and from the Puzzle Master; for this is the only time that I am touched. I seek out crying children to hold as much to comfort me as them. I get a massage every few weeks not so much to relieve my tired aching muscles which is a benefit; but so to have human contact for a few moments.

June 28, 2004

"If I had a magic wand what would you want today?" the Puzzle Master asked.

"Comfort, release from the pain and sadness," I answered. The Universe then rushed in to grant my request.

I climb up on the table and await the taking of the pulses. The room seems clouded in green and sparkles of blue. It reminds me of trying to look at the sky through the leaves of a tree. Perhaps that means wood will be the element of the day. It will be interesting to see what happens.

Unlike the previous journey I can not wait to go beyond the portal. I struggle to stay for the pulses yet I wish to be gone. The Puzzle Master is silent as she progresses through the twelve pulses. Somehow that always makes me nervous as I never know what they are telling her. What I feel is again the left middle pulse shooting energy out my little finger and the right pulses send bizarre pulsations through the right side of my body. I see the portal and can resist no longer. I am gone before the first needle is placed.

I step through the portal onto a sandy beach. Ah I thought, my sanctuary, the ocean. The waves gently lapped at the shore and then retreated back to the sea. The rhythm of the waves, the sound of the ocean comforted me. I felt at ease. I stood with my eyes closed and just listened to the symphony of the ocean. As I breathed the salt air I thought to myself, "I really expected a forest on this side of the portal, being as though the room was so green; the color of wood. But I will take the ocean any day."

I heard what sounded like a male voice behind me yet I wasn't sure as the waves made it difficult to hear. I listened closer and indeed there was a voice.

"Greetings." I heard as I turned around to find a cabin in a forest. How amazing I thought; my ideal setting; beach front mountain property. I thanked the Puzzle Master in my thoughts for arranging this incredible setting. I looked closer at the cabin trying to see where the voice originated. There on the porch was a man waving to me to come closer.

As I approached the porch I recognized him immediately. He was the Man in Blue from my previous adventures only this time he was dressed in jeans and a blue work shirt. His sleeves were rolled up to his elbows; exposing his muscled forearms. I ran to the porch and hugged him.

"I am so glad to see you." I said.

He returned with "I told you we would meet again and I always keep my promises. Come sit with me."

I turned and there before me was a willow branch bench with emerald green cushions. We sat side by side on the bench; the smell of the pine trees overhead melding with the salty ocean air below. It was as though I was in paradise. Thank you Puzzle Master. This alone has eased my pain.

As we sat on the bench he turned towards me and took my hands and began to speak, "There is a heaviness about you this day. Would you like to tell me about it?"

"I am such a pathetic fool," I said. "How can I explain to you about the cave?"

"There is no need to explain," he said. "I know of all your journeys; past, present and future."

"But how is that possible?" I asked.

"I have read them in the book yet to be written in your time. But it exists here in this space, in this time." I just looked at him unable to speak. "Do not concern yourself with that now. Please. Tell me of your heaviness," he said still holding my hands in his.

I began my saga, "Well as you know then, I found the cave of less than, of abuse. There was a polarity to that cave which I had forgotten existed. Not only did it contain the feelings of less than; it also contained its polar opposite; the desire for love. Hopes and dreams not fulfilled are once again in the Light. Dreams of a meaningful relationship. The need for human contact that I can no longer pretend does not exist. The desire to love and be loved. What good does it do to open the bud if there is no one to share the bloom with?"

He placed his hands upon my cheek and looked at me with both sadness and love in his earthy brown eyes. He gently turned me so that my back was resting upon his chest. Arms both strong and gentle wrapped themselves around me. I felt as though I were in a cocoon of pure love. He began to speak but this time his words had no sound.

"Listen and Understand. For so long you have had

your protective armor around your heart. It prevented pain from entering but it also prevented love, feelings, emotions from entering or exiting as well. Together, you and the Puzzle Master, have now removed a large portion of that armor. Beneath it is a Heart which has raw nerve endings. It is very sensitive now for it has not been exposed in many years. With the armor removed it can now feel. It feels the emotions which were locked away in the cave. Emotions that now feel strange because you have not felt them in so long."

He paused as I tried to absorb all that he said. I went inside of myself and felt my Heart. Indeed most of the armor was gone. My Heart seemed bigger; no longer confined by the armor.

"Look closer," I heard him say. I looked and looked but could find nothing else unusual and I told him so.

"Where are the reins?" he said. "The reins which you held so tightly to control your emotions?"

I began searching again. I found them hidden in the back, now longer and thinner. They were no longer pulled to the maximum tension as if they were about to break. I was amazed at their appearance.

"This is the reason you were able to cry, tears streaming down your face as you watched the moving picture. Not only have you removed the armor; you have loosened the reins. Until these tasks were completed, your dreams and wishes could not be realized. So it is that they now return. It is a sign of growth." The Man in Blue held me tighter and the cocoon of Love grew more intense.

"What of my bud, my rose?" I asked. "What good does it do to open it if there is no one to share it with? I might as well keep it in the cave."

Words without sound once again floated to my ears. "In the cave the rose can only rot and die. There, in the cave, no one will be able to enjoy its beauty, including you. It is only in the Light that the rose will bloom. Only in the Light can it be shared. Do you not see? There is an exchange between the rose and each person who passes by. Each person takes from the rose that which he needs. Some merely look at the rose; others smell its sweet fragrance while others may stroke its silky petals. But unless the rose is in the Light; the one who will see its true essence; its 'roseness,' the one who will love it will never find it. The gardener that you seek is also searching for his rose. So bloom and grow in the Light so that each may find the other when the time is right."

There was a last serge of energy through the cocoon and he released me from his arms. We sat side by side and enjoyed the ocean and the forest simultaneously. "Better?" he said now with words which could be heard.

"Yes. Better here. But on the other side of the portal it still feels sad, lonely, a little painful."

"Give it time," he said. "It is new to you. You will need time to adjust. I promise it will get better and I always keep my promises."

"Will I see you again?" I asked.

"Indeed you will. Indeed you will," he said with almost a smile on his face. It made me smile as well. "Time to go," he said. "The Puzzle Master is calling you home. I'll walk you to the portal."

We rose from the bench and walked along the shore until we came to the portal. "Peace and Love to you," he said.

"If only you could come with me to the other side," I sighed as he helped me through the portal. From behind me I thought I heard "Soon." But when I turned around he was gone; only silence remained.

The "Man in Blue," as always, told the truth. With each progressive 5 Element acupuncture treatment, with each journey of discovery and awakening; the pain eased. "Grace, Beauty, Purity and Perfection wrapped in Love" is what is now emerging onto my canvas. And the most amazing thing is that Grace and Beauty is the "original" painting. For as I awaken more and more, I see that it was the Ego which painted over the priceless Rembrandt which was me and always had been.

He was also right about this book. The proof is that you are reading it now. It sat in the potential, whole and complete for many years. I merely had to place it in the next frame of my life for it to manifest in this Earthly realm. Perhaps that is why it has taken a mere month from start to completion. It was already done before it was ever started.

Chapter 38

Surrender and Win

Shawna and I were Friends as well as acupuncturist and patient. There were grand times when we would sit outside on her patio, drink coffee and just talk. Sometimes it was easier to talk to her as a "friend" rather than as "therapist." On this particular evening she would morph two aspects of herself into one. I was confronted by my Friend as well as Samurai Healer.

Now Samurai Healer did not appear often; but when she did I knew I was in for some "tough Love." Samurai Healer did not pull any punches; she told it like it was. There was no sugar coating of any problem or situation. Although she was tough I knew that she came from a place of Love; for Love is the core of Shawna's Who. And no matter if she was Shawna, Puzzle Master or Samurai Healer that core never changed.

We sat across from each other that night, sipping coffee under the bright stars overhead. I talked of being "not good enough." Illusion Shawna countered, not true. I spoke of "not knowing enough." Again, illusion she said. She called me expert. I tried to deny it; Shawna defended it. Her strength, her words more powerful than mine defeated my every attempt to defend my position, my feelings. Only later would I learn why. From a place of total frustration, a place of total defeat I conceded to her. I said "I can't win." Had I continued Shawna would have heard that night "I give up. Uncle!" I can not fight this battle with you any longer. You win."

It seemed the foundation of that which I thought was "me" no longer existed. "Illusion all of it!" kept repeating in my mind. If that is True then "Who am i?"

I only heard sporadic sentences from Samurai Healer after that. "Get out of your head. You must face your fears. I can't do it for you. Wouldn't it be grand to speak fluently? Why do you hang on to this stuff?" I know there was more but I don't remember; my world was turning upside down.

I did not heed the Puzzle Master's advice and stayed "in my head." I could not sleep as I tried to analyze all that was said and the ramifications of it all. Finally at 5am, sheer exhaustion took over and my eyes closed in restless slumber knowing that in a few hours I would be seeing the Puzzle Master once again.

The "Man in Blue" will also be there. Over the last few months he has become my constant companion on my journeys. Always is he there to guide, to teach, to awaken me. Some times I believe he is yet another aspect of the Puzzle Master which exists beyond the portal for he is as Loving and Wise as she. And he has a name now; David.

September 12, 2004

Dearest Friend, Puzzle Master, Singer of Songs, Muse;

The events of the past night have exhausted me. I prayed that my journey this day would shed some light on this "dark night of my soul." I prayed that David would be waiting for me on the other side. I prayed that it would be the Puzzle Master who greeted me and not Samurai Healer.

The pulses once again silent, but only to me. I could feel them communicating with the Puzzle Master in ways that I myself could not. And so I prayed for a "calgone moment," TAKE ME AWAY! I never saw the portal this day, yet when I opened my eyes I was on the other side.

I felt as though I had been launched from some enormous celestial cannon. Free falling through the darkness of space I landed not in a net but upon a feather mattress. It seemed to be inside my little cabin by the sea. I could hear the waves outside the open window. Slowly David came into focus. He was sitting on the edge of the mattress holding my hand.

"How are you doing?" he said. "You certainly made an entrance crashing in here like that. I thought you were going to crash right through the bed."

"David! Thank God. I'm so glad to see you're here. I was worried that you wouldn't be here. I thought maybe you were part of the illusion too and I would never see you again. Everything seems to be in chaos at the moment. I'm not sure which end is up and which is down."

"Whoa!" he said. "Slow down. Why don't you start from the beginning and tell me what happened."

"Didn't you see and hear what happened yesterday?" I asked him.

"Yes I did. But you need to tell me what YOU heard" he countered.

"Well Samurai Healer showed up and kind of blasted me. Told me that my feelings of 'not good enough' of 'not knowing enough' were all illusion. That I was important. I tried to deny it all. Tried my best to defend my feelings but in the end Samurai Healer's words were stronger than mine. Damn it! I didn't have the words! So I told her I give up. I couldn't win the battle. I had no words to fight with. Now I seem to be in chaos. My world turned upside down. I don't know who I am any more. My foundation seems shattered."

He looked at me with his earthy brown eyes and sighed. "You need to listen yourself to the wisdom you give to others. How is it that you can be so wise when it comes to others and yet you can't see the same in yourself? You are indeed a puzzle woman."

With those words said he crawled up next to me and held me tight. I could feel the Universal rhythm of his heart beating in his chest. My own heart could do nothing but synchronize with his.

We seemed to be surrounded in a cocoon of white light with golden sparkles at the ends. The entire room seemed to glow. David began to speak, "Out of chaos comes order. This you know, for movement can not occur within stagnation and it is time for you to move. Do you know why the Samurai Healer's words were stronger than yours? Why you could not defend your words?"

"No. I tried really hard but no matter what I said I couldn't win."

"Do you think that it may have been because what she said was TRUTH? Truth needs no defense nor can it be defeated. It is your Ego not Truth which tells you of these illusions. God creates no mistakes nor does he create unimportant beings. If you are here then you are no mistake and you are important."

"But if all that I thought I was is illusion then 'who am I?' I asked.

He continued to hold me as his words poured forth "WHO you are is WHO you have always been. The Who of you has not changed. It is the WHAT of you that is changing, transforming to match your Who. Have you not told your Friend Shawna and countless others of their Who, of the God-center within them? Do you really believe that the principles apply to them and not you?"

"Now you're starting to sound like the Samurai Healer" I joked. "Okay. Okay. I give up. I give up."

"That is exactly where you need to start. Transformation is active surrender. You can not will it, or force it or demand it. You simply must allow transformation to be enacted by forces greater than yourself. Your self-talk, your Ego talk of 'unworthy,' 'unimportant,' 'undeserving' only stops the natural God force, the Universal force which is inherently in you. Don't you see this Ego talk's only function is to hide the True 'Who of you' from yourself? It is not of God this talk, for God is only Love. You are a piece of the Universal Mind of Creation. You are a piece of God. When you love and trust yourself you are loving and trusting the Wisdom that created you. When you fail to do this you are denying that Wisdom and giving the power to the Ego. There is a saying, 'You can either be a host to God or a slave to the Ego; but you can't do both.' It is only by loving yourself and respecting yourself that you connect to God and invite the energy of Creation into your consciousness, into your life."

"So by surrendering I actually win? Is that what you are saying?" I asked.

"Yes. That is precisely what is being said" David replied.

I stopped for a moment to gather my thoughts; to let his words sink into me.

"David here is my dilemma. How do I rebuild my foundation with things I don't yet feel? I am not sure I know what worthy, important, or deserving feels like."

He looked at me with sadness in his eyes as we faced each other. "The foundation has not changed. Only the 'What' of you has changed. Those feelings are around you all the time yet you do not recognize them. They feel like Kindness, Love and Respect; God's unconditional Love; the Love of your True Soul Friend; the Love of the infants you care for. They ALWAYS feel good."

"I know that in my head," I said "But my heart still doesn't believe it yet. I don't know how to live in that consciousness 24/7. Those feelings seem so foreign. So foreign that they feel uncomfortable when they do occur; as if I am wearing someone else's clothes which are 3 sizes too small. How can I change it?" I asked.

He held me even tighter and the room seemed to glow even more as he spoke. "Do not fight so hard against these feelings. Allow them to flow through you and over you. They are as new shoes; the more you wear them the more comfortable they become. Accept all complements, all acknowledgement of worthiness, importance and deserving from others with a 'thank you.' Open your Heart and ALLOW it to receive these feelings. It will get easier with time I promise."

"I hope so" I said "because right now it seems a pretty insurmountable task."

"You are important" he said. "You deserve Love and Happiness; always and forever."

I had to stop before I gave my stock answer of "Who me? You must be joking." I tried to allow his words to flow over me, to accept them in my Heart. Even though I wasn't quite there, my mind still believing in the illusion, I said "Thank you."

I could hear the Puzzle Master calling me back home, a place where illusion seems more real than the Truth. I sensed that Samurai Healer was now gone and that only the Puzzle Master awaited my return. I began to slip from the feather mattress as the portal pulled me towards it. I heard David speak as I crossed the threshold.

"I have more Faith in you than you can even imagine. Know that you can do this. Know that your Who remains intact. It has not changed. Love and trust in yourself; in your wisdom and it will light your way out of the darkness. Peace and Love to you now and always."

David told the Truth, as always. I have learned over the years that "allowing" is always better than "forcing." It is like the dog who pulls against his collar and chain strangling himself. Yet if he were to just take one step forward, to surrender as it were, he could eliminate his pain and escape from his collar.

Several years ago I was “trying” to sell my house; trying being the operative word. I did everything I knew to sell it. I got the best real estate agent, spent hundreds on advertising. I even planted a St. Joseph’s statue in the front yard because someone told me it was “suppose to work miracles.”

It wasn’t until I spoke with a friend, that I was reminded of this lesson. “Stop ‘forcing’ the sale” he said. “Simply allow God to send the perfect person to buy your house.” It is a subtle difference but an important one.

I stopped asking God and the Universe to send “Many people who are looking to buy a house;” for this is what I got; people who were looking not buying. Instead I asked “Please allow the perfect people who wish to buy this house to find it.” A different intent than my previous prayer. My house sold within the week once I ‘allowed’ the sale to take place.

Chapter 39

The Past Does Not Equal the Future

There was a different feel to the Sacred Space this day. It seemed that the energy was higher, perhaps more pure. The Puzzle Master could hear, she could feel, that which the Universe was telling her. Yet the art of seeing alluded her. It was a skill she asked the Universe and God to assist her with every day. This day her prayers were answered, for she was seeing like never before.

I on the other hand could see, could hear, yet it was feeling which alluded me. Together we worked to strengthen the areas which challenged us. The Puzzle Master taught me the art of feeling and I taught her the art of seeing.

The energy was buzzing high when I arrived that day for the Puzzle Master was seeing like never before. And for the first time I was starting to feel what the Universe was telling me.

Almost always when we enter the Sacred Space and the door is closed Shawna transforms into Teacher and I into Student. Yet this day we seemed to talk more as Friends; almost as equals, not so much as teacher and student. Even when the Puzzle Master did appear it was a more as friend. It gave a new dimension to our discussion; a level I can not remember having experienced before.

Eventually the Teacher/Puzzle Master and the Student took our places; yet the roles assumed were somehow gentler, kinder in their relationship. They had a different fell to them. It was a beautiful feeling; like angel wings touching your face or the feeling of freedom as you fly above the tree tops.

January 28, 2005

Dearest Friend, Puzzle Master, Singer of Songs, Muse, Miracle Worker;

Removal of armor was to be the order of the day. Most of it was gone yet a few pieces remained. Armor gone because of you The Puzzle Master and your talents and skill. You have succeeded where others have failed. For now more armor had been removed than remained; a victory for us both.

I climb upon the table and await the dis-armorment, but first the ritual of the pulses must be completed. First the left pulses. Your talented fingers assess and analyze each of the six pulses found there. You close your eyes, your head cocks to one side and I hear "Removal of armor" as if some map of the procedure is manifesting before you. The ritual is then completed on the right. I hear the tearing of paper as the magic needles are revealed. At the same instant I feel David's strong hand in mine.

"Time to go" he says as we are transported effortlessly through the portal.

We find ourselves seated on our bench outside the cabin by the sea. My back is pressed firmly against David's strong chest; his arms wrapped around me in a blanket of protection. We watch the waves roll across the sandy beach then recede back into the sea leaving tiny bits and pieces of foam behind.

David was the first to break the silence. "You are trembling. Are you cold? Do you need a blanket? I can get the one off the bed if you need it."

Always so attentive I thought to myself. If only I could bring him back through the portal with me. I took a deep breath and held his arms around me. "Thank you, but I'm not really cold. I'm just a little afraid right now that's all."

"Afraid of what?" he asked as if he didn't know.

"Didn't you hear? Today is dis-armorment day. I'm to have more armor removed" I said in a tone that mimicked more of having open heart surgery than a little armor removed.

"And that frightens you?" he replied. "Why? I would think you would be glad to be rid of it."

"One would think so" I said. "But in some strange way it has become a comfort to me; like an old friend. We have been through so much together, this armor and me. We have fought many battles. It has protected me from the arrows and spears of 'not good enough, freak, unlovable.' It has been there when the "other shoe fell." "I just can't seem to get rid of it all."

David turned me so that I was facing him. "My question to you is how can you not give it up. Look for yourself."

I looked deep into David's eyes as they seemed to transform into elegant mirrors. I saw in them a reflection of myself; bits and pieces of rusted armor still clinging to parts of me.

"Look closely" he said. "Sometimes we must change 'friends' in order to grow. It is time you said goodbye to this so called friend, this armor. It is old and rusted. It serves you no longer. You have out grown it in so many ways."

"But what shall I do for protection?" I asked.

"Look around you. Do you see any arrows or spears?" David asked.

I hung my head sheepishly and said "No, not now but what if…"

"There are no buts. Not any more. Mind your thoughts for thoughts become things. HEAR ME Well, THERE IS NO OTHER SHOE! You are protected by God and His infinite Love; always will be, always have been." he said. "It is only when the armor is removed that your strength, your True beauty can shine through. It is then that you are light enough to fly. It is what the Puzzle Master and Shawna have been trying to show you from the beginning for they are able to see beyond the armor. You are Beauty and Joy and Love. You are these things because you are a child of God and He is all this and more as are you."

"I understand that" I said. "I know it in my Heart but my Heart still doesn't 'KNOW' it yet. I guess my

Heart is till frightened to let it all go."

"And why do you think that is?" he asked. "Look deep, look back and find the answer."

I looked into David's eyes and saw the mirror once again. I saw myself naked before this mirror; bits and pieces of rusted armor clinging to various parts of me. What I noticed first was a rather large piece the size of a softball covering my stomach. Next I noticed another piece wrapped around the back side of my Heart. I placed both hands over the armor on my stomach and asked "Why are you still here? Tell me, show me, let me feel the reason so that I may remove you" I said out loud. Then the most remarkable thing happened.

I had closed my eyes while I recited my request yet I was now seeing a strange picture before me. It was a replica of the Norman Rockwell painting where he painted himself painting himself to infinity. Onle I was a different person in each recessive painting. In one I was a man playing a piano. In another I was a woman standing beside a man a and a little boy outside a thatched roof cottage. In two others I could see I was a Chinese doctor and a Druid Healer with Spirits dancing around my cloak. It was then that I realized these must be some of my past lives. How very cool I thought as I was compelled to step into the picture.

Once inside I felt myself being torn from the man and boy and placed in a cage. I watched as the man playing the piano had his fingers chopped off. I saw the Chinese doctor drug from his home and stabbed to death. I saw the Druid running for her life only to be dropped to the ground by an arrow piercing her back. I could watch no more and stepped out of the picture. David's strong arms were holding me once again.

"These are some of the Soul memories which you still carry with you. There are good as well as bad memories. It is why you are once again Healer; and also why you fear it so much. Know that the Past is not the Present or the Future. Please Know that this is now a different time. It is time to embrace your skills, not hide them. Armor is no longer needed. It now restricts rather than protects. It is time to let it go."

I placed my hands one atop the other, resting them on my stomach and began to pull. The armor did not move. It remained anchored to me. I pulled again with the same result. Then I heard these words in the far distance, "You can not simply rip it away. Love and Compassion will remove it."

I closed my eyes and held my hands once again over the armor as I spoke these words, "Thank you for protecting me all these years. You have done an admirable job. I appreciate all that you have done for me; but now I must ask you to leave for you see you are no longer for my highest good. It is time for me to grow, to fly!"

I felt a shaking, a vibration deep in the pit of my stomach as the armor began to lift, separate itself from my being. I pulled my hands away and there in my palm was the hunk of armor. I looked down at it in amazement.

David spoke softly into my ear, "Your Love of flying is finally greater than your fear; your need for armor. It is that Love which removed the armor. Now your bud has room to grow. Now lighter you can fly higher. A whole new world shall open up for you. Embrace it with all your Heart and Soul."

I am not quite sure what this new world will be I

thought to myself but I will do my best to embrace it. Perhaps it will be the world of writing or simply the world of feeling once again. David and I walked to the ocean's edge. He stood by my side as I threw the rusted armor into the sea. We both watched as it disappeared; carried away on the ocean's waves.

As we stood there on the beach I heard the Puzzle Master calling me home. "I guess it's time to go now. How can I ever thank you?"

David just looked at me and said "FLY!"

I awoke to the familiar voice of the Puzzle Master welcoming me home as she checked my pulses; yet I don't remember coming back through the portal. I turned just in time to see David walking back to the portal. I tried to wave "goodbye" as he left but my arms would not move. He stepped through the portal; held his arms out straight and pumped them up and down as if they were wings. "You are such a goober" I said laughing; and then he was gone.

Each moment that I drug the past with me; I recreated it once again. As a dear friend of mine once said, "It is like dragging Marley's Chain" around with you. It is just so much extra baggage that I didn't need to bring with me. It's weight so heavy there was no way that I could fly.

The armor did not protect me as I thought, but merely kept me from growth. Once I removed the armor my life bloomed. I actually talk to people now. I have met some very interesting people, with interesting lives. They have taught me wonderful life lessons that I never would have learned behind my armor.

And so I have grown.

A family, not of blood but of the Universe is now in my life because there was no armor to keep them out. They are the most loving people that I know. I don't know what I would do without them for they complement my life, my Heart and my Soul.

The world is only a 'scary' place if you make it so. You can also make it a loving and caring place if you choose. For your thoughts have energy, and energy creates your world.

Chapter 40

What I Know for Sure

This is by no means the end of my journey; but merely its beginning. Every day I learn new life lessons. Every encounter with the Puzzle Master brings new insight, new wisdom into my life. I believe that I shall learn until I depart from this shell which is my body, which houses the Who of me. Even then I believe the learning shall continue. And that every morsel of knowledge shall go with your Who wherever and whenever you choose to manifest it next.

To borrow a saying from Oprah, I KNOW FOR SURE that thoughts are energy and thus have the power to create; for <u>everything</u> is energy. That I <u>do</u> create my own world, my own 'reality.' And that it takes a different mind, a different perspective to change it than the one that created it. The most wondrous thing is that it <u>can</u> be changed.

I KNOW FOR SURE that thoughts and feelings of 'not good enough' are lies told to us by the Ego. An Ego who's only purpose is to keep us from seeing the Light and Love that we really are. 'Not good enough' is the creation of a false self based on our erroneous interpretations of life experiences. It is as Nelson Mandela has said, we are afraid to shine. I Know for sure that this serves no one, including myself. For it is in the shining, in allowing our wisdom to be shared that others as well as ourselves "AWAKEN."

I KNOW FOR SURE that the 'potential' holds within it every dream, wish and desire that can ever be imagined. And because those wishes, dreams and desires are thoughts they have energy. There is nothing that can not be manifest if you lend it your energy, your intention. Mind your thoughts for negative as well as positive thoughts come to fruition.

I KNOW FOR SURE that Blessings come in different shapes and sizes. And that often times they disguise themselves as challenges or a crisis. Now I Bless and give thanks for each challenge which comes into my life for I KNOW that at its end, just like a rainbow, there is a treasure; a divine Blessing sent from the Universe.

I KNOW FOR SURE that it is possible for buds to bloom and caterpillars to fly. It matters not the chronological age at which one starts; for time is the invention of Man not God. Know this is possible because it has been done by one. And if it can be done by one then it can be done by ALL.

If even one Being has a spark of awaken or releases even a petal of its bud for having read these words; then my vessel has served well. For I am humbled, thankful and grateful to have been the vessel through which God and the Universe have written these words for YOU!

Printed in the United States
86929LV00002B/343-528/A

9 781432 705008